Beyond Fear

The
Quantum Leap
to Courageous
Living

Fear

D0027146

Michelle Cresse

Aglow.Publications

A Ministry of Women's Aglow Fellowship, Int'l.
P.O. Box 1548
Lynnwood, WA 98046-1558
USA

Cover design by David Marty

Unless otherwise noted, all scripture quotations in this publication are from the Holy Bible, New International Version. Copyright 1973, 1978, 1984, International Bible Society. Other versions are abbreviated as follows: TLB (The Living Bible), Beck (The New Testament in the Language of Today), KJV (King James Version).

ISBN 0-932305-81-4

To my husband Gordon,
who knows how and when
to help me jump.
He believes in me.

Contents

Introduction

Can we live without fear? Would we want to? Philip Yancey, in his book *Open Windows,* titled a chapter, "In Defense of Pain." The chapter deals with the necessity of pain for functional life.

Yancey uses Dr. Paul Brand's work in a leprosy clinic to illustrate the need for pain. Dr. Brand discovered that leprosy itself did not cause rotten flesh and loss of limbs. Leprosy destroys the nervous system and prevents victims from feeling pain. When a patient is cut or bruised, he usually doesn't know it and infection sets in. "Pain itself, the hurt of pain, is a gift. After years of working with leprosy patients Dr. Paul Brand learned to exult in the sensation of cutting a finger, turning an ankle, stepping into a too-hot bath. 'Thank God for pain!' he says."[1]

Pain warns the body that it has been harmed and is in need of care. In the same way, fear is a warning. Fear is a physical and spiritual warning to watch our step. This book is not intended to make you fearless. A vast difference exists between being fearless and trusting.

Children begin their lives in an almost fearless state. At least they haven't figured out what they should fear. At age six or seven months, they crawl off any edge you happen to set them near. They put peanuts in their noses and rulers down their throats.

As kids mature, we hope they will learn enough about fear to keep them healthy. To make them hesitate at the edge of danger.

Trust is a posture. Trust is staying where God wants you, even though it's dangerous. Trust is committing yourself before you know the outcome.

You can fear and trust at the same time. In fact, the ultimate test of trust and faith is the ability to move beyond

7

your fear into the places only God can save you from.

Are you tired of fear controlling you? Do you want to be all God wants you to be? All *you* want to be?

I pray this book will help you achieve new goals and climb new heights.

1

...

Tingles and Terror

I turned off all the lights and crawled into bed. My first night home from college. My mother was at work and the rest of the family gone for the night. I was alone. My eyes closed and welcome sleep soaked into my body.

The floor creaked. No. Just my imagination and a strange house. It creaked again. A tiptoe creak. The sound stopped. My ears strained to pick up sound or movement outside my closed bedroom door. I stared hard at the shadow of the doorknob. Did it move?

I didn't breathe. I couldn't move. My hands clutched the blankets, and I prayed that whoever was in the hall would pass by my room and go on his way. A scream would never escape my mouth if an intruder attacked; my throat was locked in terror. I listened so hard my ears buzzed. Fear paralyzed everything except my heart, which pounded hard enough to make the blankets move.

By morning, I knew my ears and mind had created a monster to keep me awake. I felt foolish. But that didn't cure my leftover nausea.

The elusive monsters left me alone for years. They returned two months after my first baby was born. My husband had gone hunting, and the baby and I were alone in the house. After feeding my son, I eased into bed for the night. A wonderful, comfortable bed.

My mind drifted, my new set of mother's ears tuned in to the baby's room. But they didn't stop there. I heard a noise in the living room. Imagination again? No. It was too constant. Like something being dragged. My mind went into emergency alert. The noise was real. Without a sound, I got out of bed and put on my robe. The noises definitely came from the front room. I knew I could get to the kitchen without being seen.

"Thank you, Lord, for quiet hinges," I prayed as I opened my door far enough to slip through. I couldn't hear the noise because blood pounded through my ears. Low and close to the wall, I made my way to the kitchen and grabbed the only handy weapon. A huge meat knife in the butcher block. With a firm grasp I held the knife in front of me and moved slowly toward the living room.

My whole body felt brittle, like thin ice. A dull ache formed in my clenched jaws. Fear, terror, and anger pervaded every fiber and muscle. One thought ran in circles in my head: "You'll never touch my baby!"

I stopped. Around the corner, the grating static of the stereo mocked me and my ferocious blade. A flick of a switch, and the light came on. All was well, except my ego.

The knife was embarrassing. The inside-out robe didn't help. At least no one saw me.

I laughed at myself, put the knife away, and went to bed. No more monsters lurked in corners. No suspicious sounds pricked my fanciful ears.

A DIFFERENCE IN ME

What was the difference? In both situations I was scared to death. Even now, several years later, a fraction of the fear remains in my memory. My imagination placed me in a dangerous circumstance, and I reacted. The fear was the same. Gut wrenching. In the first situation, fear paralyzed me. If the intruder were real, my plan was to play possum. To snore, if it would help. The second time, I was ready to fight. To kill, if it would protect my baby.

The difference was not in the amount of fear or the lack of it. The difference was action *in spite of fear*.

Motivation also played a large part in the second scenario. But motivation did not erase the fear, it simply bypassed it.

FEAR ITSELF

How can a four-letter word control and extract so much power?

As human beings, we are subject to fear. In controlled doses, fear is beneficial. Even desirable. But out of control, it becomes an ornery master. Fear can run and ruin your life.

Fear is God-given; it's a reflex to keep us from snap decisions. But like everything else, Satan twists fear and uses it for his own purposes. Satan's purpose for fear in Christians is to keep us from effectively serving God.

In our physical world, fear is an intricate warning system. We don't touch a hot stove because we are afraid of being burned. We look both ways before we cross streets because we're afraid of being hit by a car. Fear, in everyday life, says, "Think before you act. Are you sure you want to do that?"

This is not the same kind of fear that pumps adrenalin into your body or makes your hair bristle. But it is fear. It's our hesitation factor, and it serves us well.

But the kind of fear we'll talk about in this book is the fear that binds. The fear that ties you up in chains and says, "You can't do that!"

The Lord wants to tell you what you can do. He wants to show you what you can do, through him, beyond fear. Not without fear, but *beyond* it. "I took you from the ends of the earth, from its farthest corners I called you. I said, 'You are my servant'; I have chosen you and have not rejected you" (Isa. 41:9) .

You are my servant; I have chosen you and have not rejected you. I have given God so many reasons to reject me. As a servant. As a child. But still he holds on and says, "I have chosen you and not rejected you."

Debbie told me about an inner battle with fear over her desire to help people.

"I'm afraid. I want so badly to be with street people. To help someone. I've even thought about selling everything and moving into a poor neighborhood; to become involved in a street ministry. I want to do something! But I'm afraid. I don't know what they'll do to me. *I'm afraid of what might happen."*

I heard more than frustration in Debbie's voice. Guilt crackled through the telephone line. We often mistake fear as sin. Or, we feel useless to God. *How can God use someone like me who is so full of fear? God needs strong, determined Christians who walk with a smile into Satan's den and strangle his minions. If I am afraid, God can't use me. Worse, he is ashamed of me.*

This is how fear becomes Satan's tool. He wants you to believe that fear renders you useless to God.

God's Word says the opposite. God wants you, fears and all. The greater your fear, the higher your calling. You are afraid because you're not stupid. If you are led by God into the jungles of Africa, your intellect says, *Hey! That's dangerous! There are snakes and natives and malaria and humongous spiders. A wild animal might eat me, or I might have to eat something disgusting like bugs!*

The first miracle in most of God's greatest plans is in the preparation of a fearful heart. In the Bible, men cast lots to know God's will. Casting lots was also a form of gambling. But God does not cast lots to choose his servants. He chooses carefully. More often than not, he chooses someone who is afraid. Someone like you.

Why would God choose you? Let's look and see. "Brothers, think of what you were when you were called. Not many of you were wise by human standards; not many were influential; not many were of noble birth. But God chose the foolish things of the world to shame the wise; God chose the weak things of the world to shame the strong. He chose the lowly things of this world and the despised things—and the things that are not—to nullify the things that are, so that no one may boast before him" (1 Cor. 1:26-29).

The people God chose to highlight in the Bible are special not for their bravery and strengths, but for their weaknesses. Even Samson, who was physically strong, was weak in character. God chose these people carefully. They are positive role models because you and I can relate to their fears. Their mistakes.

When Peter denied Jesus three times, he did so out of fear. On one hand, he wanted to know about and help

Jesus; on the other, he feared for his own life. The third time someone asked Peter if he knew Jesus, he went a little crazy. "He began to call down curses on himself, and he swore to them, 'I don't know this man you're talking about' " (Mark 14:71). He was afraid to be identified with his master.

Peter denied Jesus three times. Jesus was not ashamed of Peter or his fear. Jesus understood his heart and loved Peter for and in spite of his fear. Peter said three times, "I don't know the man!"

Not coincidentally, after the resurrection Jesus asked Peter three times: "Simon, son of John, do you love me?"

Peter's answer the third time was: "Lord, you know all things; you know that I love you" (see John 21:15-17).

WHAT ARE YOU AFRAID OF?

Are you afraid of the dark? Of being alone? Are you a mother or father whose home has become a prison for your children? Does fear of death alter or diminish your service to God? What is your greatest fear?

God has a message for you. It begins with a Bible verse you read earlier in this chapter. "I took you from the ends of the earth, from its farthest corners I called you. I said, 'You are my servant'; I have chosen you and have not rejected you. So do not fear, for I am with you; do not be dismayed, for I am your God. *I will strengthen you and help you; I will uphold you with my righteous right hand*" (Isa. 41:9, 10 italics added).

Fear is an obstacle. Obstacles can be overcome.

TIME TO CONSIDER

1. What are you afraid of? (Most of us battle multiple fears. List as many as you wish.)

2. What do you consider to be an irrational fear?

3. What causes your worst fear? (For example, an incident in your background, such as a car accident, which precipitated your feelings of fear.)

4. How does fear affect your daily life? Your spiritual life?

5. How does fear affect or interfere with your ability to serve the Lord?

2

...

God's Chicken

It's okay to be a chicken. If you're God's chicken.

The Bible admonishes us not to fear anything or anyone but God. We tend to see these verses as commands instead of encouragement. But our creator knows us, he understands our fear. After reading about Moses, I learned to admit fear. Moses was a chicken. But he was God's chicken, and that makes all the difference.

If it sounds irreverent to call a great man of God a chicken, read about his first confrontation with God in Exodus.

Everyone knows about the burning bush and the holy ground. God appeared to Moses on the mountain and delivered a stirring and passionate speech about freeing the Israelites from bondage. He ended this speech with,

17

"So now, go. I am sending you to Pharoah to bring my people the Israelites out of Egypt" (Ex. 3:10).

Did Moses jump up and say, "All right! Let's go get 'em!'"?

No. His reply was closer to mine. "But Moses said to God, 'Who am I, that I should go to Pharoah and bring the Israelites out of Egypt' " (Ex. 3:11).

God assured Moses he would not be alone. Still, Moses was not convinced. He asked a "What if?" question.

"Moses said to God, 'Suppose I go to the Israelites and say to them, "The God of your fathers has sent me to you," and they ask me, "What is his name?" Then what shall I tell them?'

"God said to Moses, 'I AM WHO I AM.' This is what you are to say to the Israelites: 'I AM has sent me to you' " (Ex. 3:13, 14).

Then God went on to make promises and plans for Moses. But Moses was afraid. He argued with God. At this point in his life, Moses was more afraid of the Israelites and Pharoah than he was of God.

Moses answered, "What if they do not believe me or listen to me and say, 'The Lord did not appear to you' " (Ex. 4:1).

God had Moses throw his staff to the ground and it became a snake. Moses ran. Was God going to use a snake to punish him for his fear? "Then the Lord said to him, 'Reach out your hand and take it by the tail.' So Moses reached out and took hold of the snake and it turned back into a staff in his hand" (Ex. 4:4) .

Next God told Moses to put his hand inside his cloak. When he took his hand out again, it was leprous. When the Lord told him to put his hand back in his cloak, his hand was healed. Even after these miracles, Moses was afraid he wouldn't be able to speak well enough for God's mission.

"The Lord said to him, 'Who gave man his mouth? Who makes him deaf or dumb? Who gives him sight or makes him blind? Is it not I, the Lord? Now go; I will help you speak and will teach you what to say'" (Ex. 4:11, 12).

After everything the Lord said and did, Moses still pleaded, "O Lord, please send someone else to do it" (Ex. 4:13).

Moses was not the picture of a confident deliverer. Yet God chose him. He didn't choose Aaron, Moses' brother who was eloquent and assured. He chose Moses. And Moses began his journey beyond fear.

PICK UP THE SNAKE

Moses' first lesson in overcoming fear was with the snake. When God changed the staff into a snake, Moses ran. He was afraid of it. The Lord could have changed the snake back into a staff as it lay on the ground, but he used it to teach Moses.

God told Moses to pick the snake up by the tail. Since Moses' first reaction was to run, I don't think he was thrilled. But he obeyed. He probably made a couple of distant grabs before he got ahold of the cold, smooth skin. Finally, he caught the tail, and it became a staff. The object of Moses' fear became less threatening in the moment he confronted that fear.

If you are afraid, God does not condemn you. He wants to help you face what you fear the most. It hurts to face what you fear. It hurts longer not to face it.

One summer, I sat on the river bank with friends from work. Some of the people had been drinking and decided to swim. One of the men went into the water with heavy boots on. His intention was to wade into the water to cool off, but suddenly he went under. He splashed and struggled. His brother, farther down river, yelled that the man

19

couldn't swim. Several of us dove into the water, fighting the current to reach him. I was the first to get close. As I extended my hand, his head sank below the surface. I stretched desperately and my fingers brushed his fingers then slipped away. He never surfaced again; we dove repeatedly, but could not find him in the muddy water.

The frustrations, the sense of failure, the fears from that summer day have stayed with me for years. One fear that lurked in the back of my mind was that I would some day come face to face with the man's widow. There was no reason why I would, or that we would know each other if we met. But the fear remained. And eight years later, the fears pervaded my dreams or kept me awake.

Finally, I sat down in the middle of the night and wrote a long letter to a friend who still lives in the area of the drowning. Part of the letter asked her to get information for me about the man's family. The rest was a mirror for my unresolved feelings. I put into words all of my fears. Then I read those words. After eight years, I understood.

I knew why I couldn't face the man's wife. At the last moment, when my fingers brushed the dying man's, I flinched. My fear reflex kicked in, and I was afraid of being pulled under. I didn't pull completely away, but it was enough that I lost his hand.

Eight years later, I was afraid to meet his wife and children because they should hate me. Surely God was disappointed in me. I was.

Fear and pain that are shoved into a corner nag but can't be dealt with. Not by you or God. But when I wrote the letter to my friend, Dianne, I brought the emotional turmoil to a level where God could deal with it. He used Dianne. She contacted the man's wife and ministered to me with love and support. She stood beside me while I grabbed for the snake's tail.

SIMPLY COMPLICATED

It sounds easy, doesn't it? Admit your fear, face it, overcome it. One, two, three. No more fears. But life on earth is not that way. Life is simply complicated. Like Moses, we make our journey to Canaan one step at a time. The steps are easy, but along the road thousands of obstacles get in the way. They complicate things.

How do we overcome fear? We begin by saying, "Boy, this really scares me." It's a relief to say it. No more pretense. No more excuses. Just a problem to be solved.

A fear need not be rational to be valid. My fear of meeting with the drowned man's widow was not rational. Even if we were thrown into the same room together neither would recognize the other. Reality did not prevent the effects fear had on me for eight years.

ARE YOU A CHICKEN?

I am a chicken. I'm afraid of thunder and lightning. I'm terrified on windy nights. I freeze at heights above ten feet. I ski, but with knocking knees. The floor boards on my side of our car have an imprint the size of my shoe. Some of my deepest fears concern my children. Nightmares come and go. At my first writer's conference, I looked for the most obscure corner of every room and occupied it. I am a chicken.

But I hear God is in the market for chickens. He wants to transform them into eagles.

TIME TO CONSIDER

For weeks after the drowning, I couldn't swim. My friends enjoyed a backyard pool, but I sat on the edge. My hand played with the water and skimmed the surface. The thought of getting into the pool brought bumps to my skin

21

and my stomach churned.

One day, Dianne's cousin threw me into the water. I was right, it was awful. Memories slammed into me and left me shaking. But I was swimming. I needed to swim.

If fear is in control of you, you'll always sit on the edge of life. You may skim the surface, but you'll never be involved. You need to swim. Risk it.

1. When was the last time you argued with God because you were afraid?

2. In what areas of your life do you stay on the "safe" edge (work, kids, romance)?

3. How have you handled fear in the past?

4. How do you think God feels about a Christian who is afraid?

5. Which has more power in your life right now, God or the situation you fear? How and why?

6. What objects or situations do you avoid because of fear?

3

...

Why Am I Afraid?

Don't think about it! Kathy silently bid her mind. Too late. The familiar knot twisted in her stomach. As she opened the car door, nausea washed through her and she staggered. Kathy felt monstrous hands tighten around her head. Screaming metal and shattering glass reverberated against her inner ears. Fear crashed into her like a gale wind. Kathy took a deep gulp of air and dove into the car as if it were water and she a diver.

Kathy deals with fear every time she enters a vehicle. Hit head-on by an intoxicated driver, after several surgeries to repair her arm, leg and collar bone, Kathy continues to wrestle with emotional scars. The fear. The helplessness. It took several months for her to get into a car on the passenger side. A year passed before she could drive again.

Coupled with the fear, Kathy was burdened by embarrassment. Friends and relatives encouraged and sometimes pressured her to ride in automobiles. But her inner agony was too great. In utter desperation she cried, "Why can't I do it? I'm so tired of being afraid! Why can't I get over this and go on?"

UNDERSTANDING FEAR

Kathy presently operates in spite of fear. She drives carefully. Memories are still present, but the edges are not as sharp. The ability to operate in spite of fear came out of a basic understanding of what terrified her in the first place.

The obvious or surface issue for Kathy was the initial accident, recorded like a gruesome movie in her mind. The images were terrifying. But the images were not the true source of her fear.

I am not afraid of death, she told herself repeatedly. *So why am I afraid?*

One day, as she took a deep breath, the movie played in her mind. The agony began, but this time, Kathy understood. It was not death she feared, but the helplessness. As she remembered the accident, she saw the red car swerve into her lane a few feet in front of her. In that frozen instant she knew. The car would hit her; she could do nothing to save herself. The agonizing knowledge of total helplessness made her feel alone and vulnerable.

Once Kathy identified the real source of her fear, she could begin to work on it. She knew that while she couldn't have saved herself, the Lord did it for her. Her car had been demolished; the engine literally sat in the front seat. Glass sprayed across the road like water, yet none had cut her. The steering wheel was bent around the

24

column, the front of the car disintegrated.

A policeman at the scene of the accident shook his head in disbelief. "Why is that woman alive?"

Kathy made progress against fear by understanding the source of her fear and the source of her deliverance.

DAVID'S FEAR

David was afraid many times. One time David felt fear because his battle reputation had preceded him. On his own, he felt helpless and lost.

David ran for his life from an irrational Saul. He ran to Gath, where the servants of Achish, the local king, said, "Isn't this David, the king of the land? Isn't he the one they sing about in their dances: 'Saul has slain his thousands, and David his tens of thousands'?" (1 Sam. 21:11).

The next verse is clear about David's reaction to these words. He wasn't proud or encouraged. Just the opposite. "David took these words to heart and was very much afraid of Achish king of Gath. So he pretended to be insane in their presence; and while he was in their hands he acted like a madman, making marks on the doors of the gate and letting saliva run down his beard" (1 Sam. 21:12, 13).

Where was the fearless David? Where was the shepherd boy who killed a giant with one stone and cut off his head? He was there, in Gath, with saliva running through his beard. Same man, different situation.

When David faced Goliath, he faced a man who mocked God. Goliath saw fear in the eyes of the Israelite soldiers every morning, and he sneered at the God of a frightened army. But Goliath had his own fears. He was a cunning bully who wanted to face one man, rather than a whole army. Every morning, Goliath, more than nine feet tall, stood up and shouted, "Am I not a Philistine, and are you not the servants of Saul? Choose a man and have him come down to me. If he is able to fight and kill me, we will become your subjects; but if I overcome him and kill him, you will become our subjects and serve us" (1 Sam. 17:8, 9).

This is called "hedging your bet." Goliath knew the tallest man in the Israelite army would probably be three feet shorter than himself. Any man brave enough to face Goliath would be sliced in two before he came within a sword's reach. In a sword or spear contest, no Israelite could match Goliath. Goliath also knew the Israelites could kill him in traditional battle if they worked together. He preferred to fight one man at a time.

When Goliath taunted the Israelites, he ridiculed God. The difference between David the giant killer and David the acting madman was motivation. David could not bear to hear God taunted.

David said to the Philistine, "You come against me with sword and spear and javelin, but I come against you in the name of the Lord Almighty, the God of the armies of Israel, whom you have defied. This day the Lord will hand you over to me, and I'll strike you down and cut off your head. . . . All those gathered here will know that it is not by sword or spear that the Lord saves; for the battle is the Lord's and he will give all of you into our hands" (1 Sam 17:45-47).

Later, when David fled to Gath, he ran for his life. He was threatened by Saul, God's anointed king. David was not defending the name of the Lord, he was defending himself. Perhaps, like many of us, David had faith in God's protection in a holy battle, but found it hard to believe during personal distress.

Motivation determines the reaction or response to fear. I believe David was motivated by his love for God and his country to act in spite of fear, and he slew the giant. In Gath, David's prime motivation was to stay alive. The depth and source of this motivation is what determined his reactions to danger.

Love for my child motivated or produced a knife wielding mother ready to slay giants in the night.

Your motivations are essential to when and how well you overcome your fears.

RATIONAL VS. IRRATIONAL

What are your motivations? Do your fears seem too inconsequential for God to intervene? Do you believe God sees your fears as valid? What *is* a valid or a rational fear?

A thin line separates rational and irrational fears. *Rational fear* can be described as the fear of possibilities. David was afraid of Achish because the King of Gath *might* perceive David as a threat and want to kill him. Kathy's fear of automobiles could be considered rational since another accident is *possible*. Her dread includes a realm of possibility.

Fear of rejection is also *rational* because it is conceivable that rejection can occur.

Actually, all fears are rational in their basic, protective form.

Irrational fear ranges from exaggerated rational fear to phobic fear. Psychologists consider phobias the number two mental health problem in the United States. According to the Living Webster Encyclopedic Dictionary, a phobia is: "A persistent, exaggerated, and usually illogical fear or dread."

Irrational fear is intense and out of proportion to the actual danger or situation. A person who experiences irrational fear often *knows* his fear is not based on logic or reality, but still he feels helpless in its grasp.

My most irrational fear is of spiders. The fear is intense and definitely out of proportion to the amount of danger I face. Black widows and poisonous spiders are not indigenous to the area in which I live. A spider can't eat me or hurt me. My mind knows that. But my ears don't.

When I encounter a spider, an intangible band tightens around my skull until my ears can't breathe. Then my ears start a low buzz that sends tingles through all my extremities. I have a very real physiological response to spiders.

Rational fear is part of the well-oiled warning system God gave us. *Irrational fear* is the result of a short-circuit in the system. It stirs physical and mental reactions in the absence of real danger.

VALID FEARS

My attitude toward spiders may seem ridiculous in view of the facts, but it is real to me. My husband cannot empathize with this particular fear because he's never had a problem with it. But his lack of fear does not affect the strength or validity of my feelings.

My fear of spiders is not a life-altering fear. But many people suffer from irrational fears that greatly restrict their quality of life. The most common phobia reported is agoraphobia, the fear of open spaces. People who suffer from agoraphobia often become prisoners in their own homes. Many have been known to go for years without crossing through the front door into fresh air.

One of the intangible locks on the door of an agoraphobic is the knowledge that no logical explanation exists for her fears. How can you make a friend or relative understand something they've never experienced? How long will friends and relatives refrain from terms such as "silly," "ridiculous," and "crazy"?

Whatever you're afraid of, you're not "crazy." If your fears interfere with normal life, you may have greater motivation to learn how to control your reactions, and eventually overcome your fears. Through the Lord, all fears can be overcome. Even the fear of death.

FEAR OF DEATH

Many Christians believe it is wrong to be afraid, even of death. Such belief is based on the knowledge of our true future: eternal residence with God. It excludes, however, our instincts for survival. John Haggai in *How To Win Over Fear,* quotes an anecdote about Dwight L. Moody:

> One day a lady asked Dwight L. Moody if he was afraid to die. He told her he was. She remonstrated with him, saying she had heard him preach that God gave grace to die.
>
> He replied, "Madam, God does give grace to die. Right now He has given me grace to live. When the time comes for me to die, He will give me grace to die." Later, Moody had a stroke and was rushed from Kansas City to his home in Massachusetts. Just before he died he said, "Earth is receding. Heaven is opening. This is my coronation day." God did give Moody grace to die as He had given him grace to live.[1]

TIME TO CONSIDER

I find it comforting that a man of Moody's stature could admit to fear of death. God does not ask us to be fearless. Only that we trust him when we're afraid. Was David afraid when he faced Goliath? Was he human? In spite of his fear, in spite of his disadvantages, David knew that God was greater than fear. Greater than circumstances. Greater than Goliath. So David could face his giant in spite of fear. Are you ready to face your fears?

1. What are your rational fears?

2. What are your irrational fears?

3. How do you feel when you're afraid?

4. Have you ever been afraid of the Lord? Why?

5. What has God asked you to do that you're afraid of?

6. What is your basic motivation for overcoming fear?

7. How can this motivation help you face your fears?

4

...

My Fear Is My Own

"My fear is my own."
He stayed in his house.
"My fear is my own."
His children watched.
"My fear is my own."
His wife withdrew.
"My fear is my own."
Friends were pushed away.
"My fear is my own."
It hurts me alone.

The way we react to problems has an effect on the world around us. The problem itself, substance abuse, anger, pain, or fear may be ours, but the impact of that problem filters out and touches many other people.

Let's start small. My fear of spiders. My fear is not a matter of life and death. I can live with it. It took several years, however, for me to realize how my fear affected my children.

If I see a spider, I move away from the area until someone disposes of it. If a spider drops on me, well, I get a little upset. I jump, yelp, and then settle down with the heebie-jeebies. (That's when you have massive shivers and say "oooooh!" a lot.)

My daughter, Nichole, witnessed a couple of my heebie-jeebie attacks, and her preschool mind absorbed my attitude. One evening, as I sat quietly beating on my sewing machine, Nichole began to scream in terror. I ran into her bedroom to find her scrunched up at the top of her bed in hysterics.

"What's the matter!" I yelled over her screams. "What happened?"

She struggled in my arms until she could point. The offender was still at the end of the bed. An ant.

"A spider!" she cried. "It's going to eat me!"

A TWISTED LEGACY

Through her own experience, Nichole had inherited my fear. The fact that an adult was afraid of tiny little spiders magnified the danger in her mind. My problem was now Nichole's.

The fact that Nichole had picked up one of my more obscure fears made me aware that she was watching me. I wondered what else she had learned from me. What had I taught her to be afraid of?

I would like to leave a better legacy with my children. I want to leave the kind of legacy Mordecai gave to his cousin Esther.

A beautiful girl, Esther was raised by Mordecai as his own daughter because her parents were killed. He brought her up in the way of the Lord and taught her many things. Esther's beauty of face and spirit was well known. Eventually, King Xerxes took her into his harem.

Esther won the favor of everyone she came in contact with, including King Xerxes. She was obedient to the king and obedient to Mordecai, who told her to keep her Jewish lineage a secret.

One of the king's officials, Haman, hated Jews. Especially Mordecai. He began a plot to destroy Mordecai and all the Hebrews throughout the kingdom of Xerxes.

The decree was made; thousands of Jews were sentenced to death. Mordecai stood by the palace gate in sackcloth and ashes, wailing his distress. He sent a message to Esther and urged her to go into the king's presence to beg mercy for her people.

Esther was afraid. First of all, the king did not know she was a Jewess. Most significantly, any man or woman who approached the king in the inner court without being summoned was put to death. If the king held out the gold scepter, the life was spared. But it had been thirty days since the king had summoned Esther. She told all of this to Mordecai in a message.

Mordecai understood Esther's fear, but he sent back this answer: "Do not think that because you are in the king's house you alone of all the Jews will escape. For if you remain silent at this time, relief and deliverance for the Jews will arise from another place, but you and your father's family will perish. And who knows but that you have come to royal position for such a time as this?" (Esther 4:13, 14).

Esther asked Mordecai and all the Jews in Susa to pray and fast for three days. She and her maids also prayed and fasted. Afterward, she went to the king even though it was against the law.

With a shrug of her burdened shoulders, she accepted the unknown. "And if I perish, I perish" (Esther 4:16).

A WORTHY LEGACY

Mordecai taught Esther an important lesson on fear. In a sense, he asked Esther, "What's the worst that could happen?"

He was telling Esther to order her priorities. He made no promises for her safety, guaranteed no reward or success. He simply urged her to obey. To act in spite of fear.

Esther took the time to pray and fast; then she went into action. Esther, in the move beyond her fear, defeated Haman's plans. He was hanged on the gallows he built for Mordecai.

I want my children to learn to live beyond fear. I want them to know that even a heart filled with fear has room for faith. It's our mustard seed of belief.

Mordecai, with the ashes of fear and distress upon his head, told Esther: "For if you remain silent at this time, *relief and deliverance for the Jews will arise from another place*" (Esther 4:14 italics added).

Mordecai's ultimate faith was in God, not Esther or himself. He was concerned, anguished by events, but underneath his anguish was a mustard seed planted by God. He knew, regardless of Esther's choices, that the Jews would be delivered.

Surrounded by the best of everything and recipient of incredible luxuries, Esther was safe and happy in the harem. In one small action, one fleeting moment of time, she could lose everything, including her life. She took the step.

Esther walked into the throne room. She was not motivated by self-confidence. She held her breath as the king, astounded, watched her approach. The room became hushed. But the king was pleased with Esther and held out the gold scepter that was in his hand.

Esther's life hung in the balance the moment she stepped into Xerxes' presence. But if she had given into her fears, it would have affected thousands of people. One step brought her into the throne room of history.

EVEN IF HE DOES NOT ...

God delivered Esther and her people in the eleventh hour. As most of us face difficult problems, we hear a tiny voice in the back of our mind that says, "At the last moment, God will take over." But sometimes it doesn't happen the way we think it will.

Three young boys were forced to make a decision similar to Esther's. They had to choose between God and survival. Would God snatch them away from harm?

Shadrach, Meshach, and Abednego wouldn't bow down and pay tribute to a golden image of King Nebuchadnezzar. The enraged king ordered them: "Now when you hear the sound of the horn, flute, zither, lyre, harp, pipes and all kinds of music, if you are ready to fall down and worship the image I made, very good. But if you do not worship it, you will be thrown immediately into a blazing furnace. Then what god will be able to rescue you from my hand?" (Dan. 3:15).

The answer given by the young men facing a mighty king shows an incredible knowledge of priorities. They said: "If we are thrown into the blazing furnace, the God we serve is able to save us from it, and he will rescue us from your hand, O king. *But even if he does not, we want you to know, O king, that we will not serve your gods or*

35

worship the image of gold you have set up" (Dan. 3:17, 18 italics added).

Nebuchadnezzar was not as understanding as Xerxes. He was furious with the boys' stubborn faith. He had the furnace stoked until it was seven times hotter than usual (he had never heard of over-kill). Then the three boys were thrown into the fire. Even the soldiers who pushed them into the fire were incinerated instantly by the heat. But Shadrach, Meshach, and Abednego were spared.

I can't help but wonder if certain thoughts crossed their minds as they watched the fire intensify. Thoughts like, "Hey, God's really going to let us be thrown in there!" Maybe they waited for a bolt of lightning to strike Nebuchadnezzar before their sentence was carried out. But they were thrown into the furnace.

God sent a companion of comfort and praise. Part of my admiration for Shadrach, Meshach, and Abednego comes from their humble spirit of obedience. When Nebuchadnezzar saw what was happening in the furnace he yelled, "Shadrach, Meshach and Abednego, servants of the Most High God, come out! Come here" (Dan. 3:26).

If *I'd* been walking around in that furnace, I would have been tempted to say, "Come and get us!"

But they were obedient and came out of the furnace.

Can you?

OUT OF THE FURNACE

One sure way to avoid your fears is to lock yourself in. Use your house, your closet, or your mind. But as you hear the bolt slide into the lock, consider what's on the other side of the door. Family. Friends. Life.

Shadrach, Meshach, and Abednego had a wonderful time in the furnace. An angel accompanied them as they sang praises to God. But when the king asked them to come out, they stepped through the opening of the furnace. They came out to be living examples of God's strength.

In the furnace, three boys found comfort and safety in the presence of God. Absolute security. When King Nebuchadnezzar called them out you might say they jumped out of the fire into the frying pan. They came back to the world of human unpredictability. They returned to serve a man who wanted them dead only moments before. They fulfilled their responsibilities.

FEAR AND RESPONSIBILITY

Sheri walked with her seven-year-old son to the heavy carved door. "Good-bye, Paul." She smiled. "Walk with God."

With a kiss and a wave, Paul ran for the school bus. Sheri closed the door and leaned back against it. "Please, Lord, walk with Paul. Protect him."

Her thoughts churned. Every school day began with fear and ended with sweeping relief as Paul clambered off the bus.

Sheri and her husband Jim were missionaries in the Philippines during the height of the revolution. Their house was in Manila, and Paul rode a school bus for two hours a day on streets that could erupt with violence at any moment. Sheri's maternal instincts screamed for the protection of her child.

One morning the fear became too powerful. "Lord, I want to keep Paul home," Sheri prayed. "There are shootings, flash floods, the brakes on the bus go out, and Paul's asthma is so bad. He's only seven, Lord. I'm afraid. I can't be a responsible mother and put him on that school bus every day."

A quiet moment followed her prayer. In her heart, she heard God's words. "Sheri, it is responsible for you to put Paul on the bus five days a week. It's responsible because it is what I require of you. For now."

He gave no promises of safety. He just let her know that the best and faithful thing for her to do was to let go each morning. From that day on, she could let go of Paul. As she did, she relinquished her fear. God was responsible.

You are responsible first to God, then to your family, then to the people in your world. Fear hurts you, and it hurts all of them. As long as you give in to fear, you will never accomplish what God has for you to do. God can and will find other people to do what you will not, but he wants you.

TIME TO CONSIDER

In Miriam Adeney's book, *A Time For Risking,* she discusses Esther's story, then encourages the reader to ask herself: "What have I come to the kingdom for?"

Ask yourself the same question. Then consider Miriam Adeney's evaluation of the answer:

It isn't enough to know what's right. Beyond that, we need energy and courage to do what's right. We need motivation. That comes as we let ourselves be filled with God's word, like Jeremiah. As we wait upon the Lord, praying over his Word day by day, our spirits are renewed and we soar up like eagles (even though we work with turkeys!). Instead of gritting our teeth and plodding on, we fly.[1]

Jump out of the fire into the frying pan. Enter the throne room. Feel and savor the tingle that runs up and down your spine as you discover, "What have I come to the kingdom for?"

1. What is your place of comfort and safety? Are you ready to leave it?

2. Define fear. Define "lack of faith."

3. Esther said, "If I perish, I perish." Shadrach, Meshach, and Abednego said, "But even if he (God) does not (save us) we will not worship your gods." Was this lack of faith? What did they mean?

4. How do your fears affect your relationship with God?

5. How do your fears affect your family?

6. How do your fears affect your friends?

7. How has fear affected your ability to function?

5
...

How High Can a Chicken Fly?

My chickens can fly. Well, not really fly. They kind of take a flying leap. I've watched them. They squat down real low, then they jump as high as they can and flap their wings in a mad imitation of a fat bird. Once in a while one of the hens will fly high enough to clear the top of the chicken wire.

I haven't quite figured out *why* they work so hard to leave the chicken coop. Usually, the befuddled fowl spends the next couple of hours scratching around the fence trying to get back in.

How high can a chicken fly? Our chicken fence is about seven feet high, so they can go at least eight feet. But can they go higher? If they can, why don't they?

Chickens are equipped with the ability to fly. When

severely threatened, they will take to the air for a short flight. The landing is less than graceful; often accomplished with a comical somersault of feathers and irritated squawking.

They possess the ability, so why are they on the ground when they could soar, dip, and dive? I turned to my husband one night and pulled an odd question out of the hat. "Gordon, why can't chickens fly?"

Gordon shrugged his shoulders (he's almost used to my strange questions). "They probably can. But they don't need to."

He was right. Chickens have a nice life. From the first day out of the egg, their food, water, and clean straw are provided. Eat, scratch, sleep. What more could they want? Their bodies grow fat; their wings become extra appendages. Flight is a mere survival instinct.

I was a chicken content with safety and comfort. But somewhere, hidden under the rock of my subconscious, was the desire to fly.

A dream was born in high school. I mentioned it to my husband when I turned twenty-nine. "Before my thirtieth birthday, I want to jump out of an airplane."

"Why?" Gordon asked. "Don't you like living here?"

My desire to skydive was rooted in fear. I'm afraid of heights, and small planes make me shiver. But I needed to prove to myself that I could do it. Make that final step.

Gordon encouraged me to take a skydiving class. The class and the first jump took one day. All through the class, I shook my head. *I'm nuts,* my mind rotated. *I can't do this.*

In class, the instructor listed nine things that could go wrong, and what to do if one or all of them happened.

"You jump out of the plane, count to six and check your chute. The parachute may not deploy, the lines may be tangled, a cell may not inflate . . . here are some steps to remedy most emergencies. . . ."

"This guy really thinks I'm going to remember all this while I spiral toward the ground, hundreds of feet per second," I muttered under my breath.

"If all else fails," the instructor intoned, "pull the reserve chute." Of course, once you pull the reserve chute, you go through the nine steps again to see if this one works. The odds of both chutes failing are a thousand to one. "But hey . . ." The cavalier educator laughed. "Stuff happens." Reassuring.

After the class, the instructor led our group of shaking would-be jumpers onto the airfield to practice exiting the aircraft. The instructor sat in the doorway of a rickety, grounded airplane and explained the step-by-step procedure:

"You will be sitting in the doorway, next to the jumpmaster. He will attach your static line to the floor of the airplane. You will test it. The jumpmaster will tell you to turn in the door so your feet are on the step, and you are facing out of the airplane."

Uh uh, I thought. *Sit in an open doorway at three thousand feet? Uh uh!*

The instructor's voice went on. "You will plant your feet firmly on the step, and on the jumpmaster's command, grab the wing strut with both hands and heave yourself out of the craft. Cross one foot over the other until only one foot is on the step. The right foot is held behind the left foot."

Hey! I can't fly around at three thousand feet with one foot on a six inch wide step holding onto the little wing strut of a mechanical mosquito!

The only thing that kept me from running for my puny life were Gordon's words in my memory. "I don't want you to say on your seventieth birthday, 'I shoulda done it.' "

Those words and the fee I paid for the class kept me in jump school. Half of me gave rapt attention, while the other half shook her head no. Sanity begged, *I don't need this. I can't do this.*

THE FIRST STEPS

The first step in overcoming any problem is the same: Admission. Before you can tackle fear you have to know that you're afraid, and you need to know why you're afraid. I have a friend who is good at making me dig into my feelings.

We'll have a nice, casual conversation, and I'll make a comment like: "I'm afraid of thunderstorms."

My friend turns and says, "Why?"

My first answer is often, "I dunno." (I don't talk like a writer.)

"Think about it. There's got to be a reason."

I don't always want to dig into my past or my emotions; it's hard, painful work. But when I've made the effort, it's always worth it. Knowing why you are afraid can provide excellent motivation for moving beyond fear.

The second step down the road of trepidation is instruction. It helps to learn and absorb as much information about a problem as you can find. This process is especially helpful because you discover others out there with the same fears you have. It won't take away the fear, but the company helps.

So I went to ground school. Fear is too mild a word to describe my feelings during the class. I was alternately sick, dumbfounded, and angry for what I had gotten myself into. My instincts screamed in every inch of my quaking body, *Leave! You idiot!*

But something, somewhere (probably my big toe), a part of me wanted to stay. To conquer myself. My fear.

I didn't run out on a certain Saturday and jump out of an airplane. I planned ahead, registered for a class, and spent the necessary time to prepare for my big leap. Fools jump without guidance and instruction.

GIDEON

One of the most cautious men in the Bible was Gideon. He could never be accused of jumping without guidance. In fact, he couldn't be accused of jumping. His pace was measured and calculated.

The first time God met with Gideon he said, " 'Go in the strength you have and save Israel out of Midian's hand. Am I not sending you?'

'But Lord,' Gideon asked, 'how can I save Israel? My clan is the weakest in Manasseh, and I am the least in my family' " (Judg. 6:14, 15).

The Lord reassured Gideon, but even so Gideon began the tests. Gideon tested God a total of three times before he went to war against the Midianites. Each test had a positive result, but Gideon was still afraid. And God knew it.

He said: "If you are afraid to attack, go down to the camp with your servant Purah and listen to what they are saying. Afterward, you will be encouraged to attack the camp" (Judg. 7:10, 11).

Finally, Gideon was able to do God's bidding.

The best thing Gideon ever did was to seek God's reassurance in the midst of his fears. His fears were powerful. He was afraid of his father and the people who lived in his town. He was afraid of the mighty Midianite army. He was afraid to be a leader.

Rather than deny his fear or hide because of it, Gideon confessed to the Lord and asked for reassurance. But God didn't erase Gideon's fears all at once. Instead, he used those fears. And Gideon was not alone. "The Lord said to Gideon, 'You have too many men for me to deliver Midian into their hands. In order that Israel may not boast against me that her own strength has saved her, announce now to the people, "Anyone who trembles with fear may turn back and leave Mount Gilead.' " So twenty-two thousand men left, while ten thousand remained" (Judg. 7:2, 3).

Two thirds of Israel's army trembled with fear. Twenty-two thousand men. I wish I could have been there when the announcement was made. How long did the army stand, silently staring at their feet waiting for the first man to build up the courage to step out and say, "I'm trembling"? Why didn't Gideon leave? He was afraid. When twenty-two thousand men returned home, why wasn't Gideon with them?

Gideon was different. He took the time to ask instructions from God. He waited for confirmation. He wanted to be sure that God was saying, "Yes, Gideon, it's you I want." Then, step by step, God revealed his plan to Gideon. And step by step, Gideon followed, albeit trembling.

From the beginning God knew he would send three hundred men to defeat an army as thick as locusts and whose camels "could no more be counted than the sand on the seashore." (Judg. 7:12)

But the Lord didn't say to Gideon, "Just take three hundred men." A long process occurred before three hundred men remained.

START WALKING

Take the first step. Seek God. What are you afraid of? Tell God about the fear. Then wait for his instructions. Accept his reassurances. Let him pat you on the back and say, "It's okay. Let's do this together." One step at a time.

Kay has learned about the tiny steps to freedom. She was literally locked in her house for three years. Seized by incredible panic attacks even from talking on the telephone, Kay came to the point of suicide. When family members brought her food, she hyperventilated in the grips of irrational fear and panic.

One afternoon, Kay called out to God. "Help me!" she sobbed. "I can't go on like this! If you are there, God, help me! Help me or let me die."

The phone rang. Kay picked up the receiver but couldn't speak. The caller identified herself. "My name is Marjorie. I was an agoraphobic. I know you're afraid. We can beat this, Kay. Together. We're going to bring you back into life. This is the first step. Tomorrow I'll call again, we'll talk longer. Each day we'll do a little more."

Kay slowly lowered the receiver. Adrenalin still pumped through her body from a panic attack, but hope flowed with it. She wasn't alone. Someone else understood.

Every day, Kay took a new step. Now, a year and a half later, Kay picks up the telephone and dials. Someone answers, and Kay says, "My name is Kay. I was an agoraphobic. I know you're afraid. . . ."

GROUND SCHOOL

Kay attended the same school as Gideon. God's ground school. To prepare for my great leap, I attended a ground school. Kay, Gideon, and I wanted to quit school and stay on the ground, in the chicken coop, but God had other plans.

How are your wings? Have they grown useless because you haven't needed them? Get into God's ground school. Seek his reassurance. Step by step, exercise those wings. Don't be content to survive. Fly. Rise up with eagles.

TIME TO CONSIDER

Take time today and tomorrow to make your first step beyond fear. Don't try to completely overcome it. Instead, creep up on it and nibble a piece off. (I'm not suggesting you eat spiders or anything.) If you're afraid to speak in front of groups, check out books from the library about public speaking. If you're afraid to drive, sit in a car for half an hour. If your fears are based on thought, read and reread Joyce Landorf's decision about her own "Dark Thoughts": "I can expose the Dark Thoughts for exactly what they are: tragedies that haven't yet happened. And I can choose to let that knowledge control my responses to those thoughts."[1]

1. What is your motivation for overcoming your fear?

2. What can you do now that would be a first step toward flight from fear?

3. What makes you want to turn back?

4. Who are the people you might learn from? Do you know others who have gone through similar difficulties?

5. When will you start ground school? When will you make your first efforts in overcoming fear?

6. What reassurances has God given you when you were afraid?

7. What would be the best reassurance you could receive from the Lord?

8. What are you learning in ground school? What are you using for a textbook?

6

. . .

On the Wing

After I shook my head no for five hours, ground school
was over. The jumpmaster fit me for a parachute and
strapped me in. He kept fiddling with some knob. Every
couple of minutes he'd yell over his shoulder, "Hey, Karl!
This thing isn't working."

Finally, after turning the knob for ten minutes, he said,
"Ah, forget it" and turned to the next jello-jumper. His
concern for my life was touching.

The parachute was heavy and awkward. I was mortified
at the thought of taking the last step of my life in a bell-
bottomed jumpsuit. I'd be a '70s-style blob on the ground.

We approached our plane. Jump instructors make every
effort to encourage their students to complete their jumps.
Obviously, quite a bit of that effort went into the aircraft.

Fabric hung in tatters from battered aluminum walls. A window was cracked, and only the pilot enjoyed an actual seat. As I crawdad-crawled into the tail section, I realized only a fool would want to land in this plane. The idiots jump out. Somewhere in between was the pilot.

We taxied down the runway as my husband and children waved good-bye. Nothing seemed real. My head entered a fog with a mournful horn sounding in the background. It echoed, "Why, God? Why, God?"

The pilot and jumpmaster carried on light banter while the two other jumpers and I stared out the window and tried to find enough fluids in our mouths to swallow.

At three thousand feet, the first jumper climbed out of the airplane and dropped with a loud, "Oh, noooooo!" Within seconds the metal clip at the end of his static line jerked, then whipped and banged against the airplane.

"One away!" the jumpmaster yelled with glee. He closed the door and helped the second jumper get into position beside the pilot.

In a few minutes, too few minutes, the static line beat against the thin sides of the airplane, and the jumpmaster yelled, "Two away!" He closed the door and turned to me.

"Okay, Michelle. Get into position." He helped me maneuver my pack between the pilot and the door. With both hands, I gripped the side of the pilot's seat. I would say my knuckles were white, but sometime after the first jumper fell my blood stopped pumping, so my whole body was colorless. I hoped the two men couldn't see how frightened I was.

"Michelle." The patient jumpmaster smiled. "Why don't you let go of the pilot's chair? We wouldn't want you to take him with you."

He opened the door and the wind roared around us. A hand patted my knee, and I heard the jumpmaster yell over the noise, "I'm in the army! When I took my first jump, my sergeant told me: 'Macho is not being fearless; it's doing what you're afraid of!' I never forgot that! What you're doing is macho. You're doing what most people want to do, but are too afraid."

Great! I thought. *Will Gordon still love me if I'm macho?* I realized the plane didn't look so bad after all. A little paint, a new window, some body work. . . .

Then I heard those dreaded words: "Michelle, put your feet on the step and get out."

Obediently, I put my feet out and braced them against the tearing wind. My hands, one at a time, reached to grasp the narrow wing strut. A dozen pleas, a thousand thoughts, flashed through my mind, but the only one I remember is, "I can't."

My arms didn't hear my head, and they pulled my unwilling heart outside the plane. I was flying at three thousand feet on one foot. My hands held the wing strut so tight I was afraid it would buckle. A seventy mile an hour wind ripped at my precarious position.

I was totally numb, paralyzed, and nauseated by terror.

GET OUT ON THE WING

During the ground school, our instructor made the class a promise. He assured us that we would not be forced to jump. If we changed our minds, we would be allowed back into the airplane. "We've only had to make one extraction," he said. "The guy was so paralyzed they couldn't get him back in the door, so they pried him off the plane and let him drop. He did fine."

As I waited for the order to get on the step, I considered my options. I didn't have to jump. But a lot was at stake. My dreams. My fear. My self-respect. My husband's respect. Ninety-two dollars.

I had to get out of that airplane. Was my need to jump rooted in flinches of the past? I'm not sure. But I needed to know I could leave the airplane. Even as I stood on the step, I didn't really think I would jump. Yet as I climbed out the door, faced the wind, and inched out to the edge of the step, I came face to face with my fear. And one step into it.

The most difficult step I have ever taken in my life was the one out of the plane. I deliberately decided to put myself in a position of danger. The men and women at the air field make several jumps a day, hundreds per year. They say the danger is relative. But to my uninitiated mind, the danger was directly related to me.

I was numb, terrified, paralyzed. But there was also a tiny spark of jubilation. If you want to move beyond your fears, you will be forced to make formidable decisions. Some of those decisions will put you on a path to physical or emotional danger.

What kind of airplane are you flying in? When you're safe on the ground, it looks pretty terrible. But when the time to jump comes, the ol' plane takes on a new shine. It's not so bad. The temptation to stay where you feel safe is strong. Sometimes undeniable. "I can always overcome my fears some other time. I'll just stay here, for now."

A flinch. And it will haunt you until you move out of your safety zone. Make your decision. Face the wind. Take a drink of satisfaction over your first small victory.

TAKING STEPS

The first two steps in moving beyond your fears are:

1. *Admission.* Admitting to yourself and God that you are afraid.

2. *Ground school.* Seeking guidance from the Lord. If you're afraid of confrontations, take a class designed to

help you develop assertiveness. Get instruction. The more you know about the object of your fears, the less threatening it is.

The third step is tough. Many people climb the first two steps without loss of breath. But number three is a doozy. This is the step that makes a commitment.

3. *Get out of the plane.* Brace yourself against the winds of panic. Take the step that puts you in the direct path of your fears.

Many people find it hard to believe that Jesus experienced fear. But Luke tells about Jesus' prayers on the Mount of Olives. "He withdrew about a stone's throw beyond them, knelt down and prayed, 'Father, if you are willing, take this cup from me; yet not my will, but yours be done.' An angel from heaven appeared to him and strengthened him. And being in anguish, he prayed more earnestly, and his sweat was like drops of blood falling to the ground" (Luke 22:41-44).

When he was physically born into our world, Jesus inherited the same reflexes we possess. His flesh contained nerve endings created to feel pain and discomfort.

As the Son of God, Jesus knew exactly what was in store for him. He knew the levels of pain he would experience. And because he dared to become one of us, he feared as we fear.

Above and beyond his knowledge of the imminent physical pain, Jesus knew he would suffer the agony of a soul steeped in sin, cut off from God. Fulton J. Sheen, in *Life of Christ*, strives to give his readers a look into what he termed, "The Agony in the Garden." As he describes this most excruciating episode in the life of Jesus, a fraction of the misery pierces our veiled understanding about why Jesus was afraid.

From the North, South, East and West, the foul mi-asma of the world's sins rushed upon Him like a flood; Samson-like, He reached up and pulled the whole guilt of the world upon Himself as if He were guilty, paying for the debt in our name so that we might once more have access to the Father. . . .To most men, the burden of sin is as natural as the clothes they wear, but to him the touch of that which men take so easily was the veriest agony.[1]

Jesus' body and soul writhed in fear and pain with the knowledge of the guilt he would bear on the cross.

What did he do when he was afraid?

1. *He admitted it.* "Father, if you are willing, take this cup from me . . . ."

2. *He went to ground school.* He prayed and allowed an angel of God to minister to him and strengthen him.

3. *He stepped out.* Jesus saw the soldiers and religious leaders coming to arrest him. Did he run? Did he hide? No.

"Jesus, knowing all that was going to happen to him, *went out and asked them*, 'Who is it you want?' 'Jesus of Nazareth,' they replied. 'I am he,' Jesus said." (John 18:4, 5 italics added).

John's phrasing here is interesting. "Jesus, knowing all that was going to happen to him, went out and asked them. . . ." In the midst of utter fear, pain, and soul-agony, Jesus stepped out to meet the men who would deliver him to the cross.

To say that Jesus felt fear is not an attack on his deity. It is recognition of the extent he went to in order to become one of us. "For this reason he had to be made like his brothers in every way, in order that he might become a merciful and faithful high priest in service to God, and that he might make atonement for the sins of the people" (Heb. 2:17).

Jesus understands our fear because he felt the concentrated torrent of fear. Fear that made his sweat like drops of blood. God responded to the anguish of his Son. He sent strength and courage that enabled Jesus to step out in front of the men who would abuse him and say, "Who is it you want? I am he."

GET OUT, GET OUT, WHEREVER YOU ARE . . .

The hardest thing to do when you are in the grips of panic is to think straight. I guess that's why I stood outside the airplane with my eyes closed and a death grip on the wing strut. A thought kept playing through my mind: *What if I fall, what if I fall, what if I fall?*

I had a parachute. Really, the whole idea was to fall. At that point, I wasn't worried about a faulty chute, or bad winds. I was afraid of falling. So are you. We hate to be out of control. But falling is not the worst thing that can happen.

The worst that can happen is to find yourself saying, "I should have."

When I think about the man I saw drown, "should have's" plague my mind. I know the man's wife holds no hard feelings for me. Other people will always rationalize and say, "Michelle, you can't change what happened. It wasn't your fault."

But in my mind, "should have's" live on. Can you live with them?

I know a girl with a beautiful singing voice. Someone sent a tape of one of her songs to a recording company. The record company was impressed enough to send a letter asking her to audition for one of their representatives. The girl was excited but extremely shy. She was enveloped in terror. As the time drew closer for the audition, my friend's fear grew until she was frantic. Two days before her appointment she called the representative and canceled the audition.

Regret poured out as she told me about this missed opportunity. "Michelle, I should have done it. What's the worst that could have happened? They might have said no, and I would have been no worse off than I was before. But now I'll never know."

I'M SO AFRAID

A boy named Eric woke up one day and looked out the window. In the backyard he saw the tree house his father built for him. He wanted to climb the great oak tree and play in the wonderful house in the branches, but every day he thought, *What if I fall? I'm so afraid.*

Eric grew taller, his voice deepened, and stubs of hair grew upon his smooth chin. He was proud of the letter he received offering him a college scholarship, but a tape recorder played in his mind, *What if I fall? I'm so afraid.*

Eric became a man; he had a good, steady job. He even took a few college courses at night. He wanted the promotion his boss offered him. Better pay. His own office. He might even think about getting married, since he would have more security. But he thought, *What if I fall? I'm so afraid.*

Eric sits by the window. His hair is white, his fingers curled, he wears slippers instead of shoes. Eric doesn't need shoes. His doctor keeps telling him his legs will grow worse every day that he doesn't walk, but Eric sits by the window, just staring. From his soft, overstuffed chair, Eric can see a tree house. The great branches of the old oak still support and surround the house, but the wood is gray. Boards have fallen off on one side. Eric shifts in the chair and sighs. "I suppose I ought to go for a walk," he says. "But . . . what if I fall?"

TIME TO CONSIDER

What a beautiful view from my tiny perch at three thousand feet. The countryside I had lived in for six years looked completely different. This perspective gave my old boondocks a new face. A vivid and incredible face. My first gaze at this new world was through the cracked and scratched Plexiglas of the airplane window. The startling colors were dull and whitened by the old plastic.

If I had stayed in the airplane, I would never have seen the entire fantastic panorama; my perspective confined to what I could see through the ten-inch window. One narrow vision.

Every step we take into and beyond our fears enlarges our vision. Our horizons are shoved back.

The most difficult step I have ever taken was the one that brought me out of my airplane. It was also a most important step.

1. What kind of airplane are you flying in? Where do you feel safe?

2. Why do you feel safe there?

3. What is security? What does your security depend on?

4. God led Moses and the people of Israel to a land of milk and honey. Describe the path they followed to reach this land. Was the path safe? How did it affect their sense of security?

5. What "should have's" do you have in your past?

6. What can you do about the past?

7. What do you want to do about the future?

8. What is the next step you must take to move beyond your fear?

9. When will you take that step?

7
...
Look at the Jumpmaster

In the movies when someone is high in the air, a shout is always heard from below: "Don't look down!"

As I strangled the airplane's wing strut, my toes gripped the metal step through my boots, and I looked down. It wasn't scary at all. It was beautiful. But I *was* terrified to look back at the door of the airplane. I knew if I looked I would see the jumpmaster. He would see me look at him. That's the signal that a jumper is ready for the "Go!" command.

I looked down. I looked up. Off to my right were some gorgeous mountains. Above me were blue skies. I could take this view in for the rest of my life. Was this the rest of my life?

Eventually I had to look at the jumpmaster. It would be

a shame to let the plane run out of gas and leave these nice guys in a lurch.

My fingers tightened their tenuous hold on the cool metal. I heard something grinding and realized my teeth were getting shorter. Slowly, my head turned to the left. The last resort was to beg with my eyes for the man in the open door to say, "Come on back!"

The jumpmaster smiled slyly and waved a little salute. Then he yelled, "Go, Michelle!"

THE BEST VIEW

The old adage "Look before you leap" is excellent advice. But where do you look? For me, as a parachutist, the best place I could look was at the jumpmaster. In fact, it was vital for my survival.

I could have, theoretically, jumped without the jumpmaster's signal. An extremely foolish move. The jumpmaster had an unrestricted view of the target. He could see the the windsock below and knew the wind direction. His proximity to the pilot kept him informed on the aircraft's speed. His training and experience wrapped all these pieces of information into a tidy package that said, "If we can get her off the wing now, she might land near the target area."

The target we beginners aimed for, a large horse pasture, should have been easy to hit. But people who jumped too soon or too late made some spectacular landings. One man landed in the backyard of a house a mile from the field. Another man landed on the roof of a house. A young girl almost made it. She landed in the top of the trees next to the pasture. She wasn't injured, but the fire department had to rescue her from the lofty landing site.

All of these mishaps resulted from not looking at the jumpmaster or sluggish obedience when they did look. In a moment of extreme fear, they grasped for control instead of investing their trust in the one who could help them.

A DELICATE TRUST

We human beings find it difficult to transfer trust from ourselves to another. Most adults prefer to drive a car as opposed to being driven because of a need to control. When my husband drives, I watch red tail-lights flash up ahead as a driver steps on the brake and find myself applying the passenger brake. While I have faith in my husband's driving ability, I experience the slightest thread of doubt that he sees the brake lights or that he will respond in the way I would. My subconscious wants to exert control, so my foot slams through the floor board.

In the same way, the greatest struggle we face is over control. We aren't sure what God will do if we give him total control, so we hang on to the steering wheel.

In high school I had a close friend who wasn't a Christian. We had many long discussions about God, Jesus, and her needs. She acknowledged the existence of God, the birth of Jesus, and the one and only way to eternal life. But our discussions usually ended with her admission: "I'm just not ready to give up yet."

For my friend, "give up" meant letting go of control of her life. To her, Jesus was not salvation, but restriction. She was afraid that by accepting Christ as Savior, she would have to give up many of the things she enjoyed. She was not ready to concede that kind of control in her life.

She couldn't see where the road of self-control would lead. After years of pain, heartache, and poor decisions, my friend decided to look at the Jumpmaster. She waited in the tree tops of self-direction while he brought the ladder truck to rescue her.

When I went to my ten year high school reunion, I

looked for an unoccupied corner where I could watch people come in. I was in my corner at the far end of the restaurant talking to a nameless face from my past when I heard this wonderful shriek from the doorway.

"Miiichelle!" Coe ran through and over anyone in the way. "Michelle! I've been looking for you for months!" She wrapped her arms around me in a bear hug. "I've accepted Christ!"

Coe and I held our own reunion that night.

Why did it take so long? Why did she have to go through so much pain before she could admit her need for the Lord? Because she was just like me. She was afraid to look at the Jumpmaster because he might give her the "Go!" command. And she didn't want to hear it.

Jesus is the only jumpmaster who is qualified to exert control in your life. His view is unrestricted. Is yours? He sees what you have gone through in the past. He knows what you face right now. Past, present, and future form one large picture before him. Only he is trained to observe the details and draw conclusions. What can you see?

You see the past through murky windows that allow only the brightest vignettes to show through. Your perception of the past distorts your view of the present as well as your hopes for the future. Beyond the hopes, the future appears as empty space. And even if you could see as Jesus does, you do not possess the wisdom and ability to translate them into the tidy package of direction.

Do you really want to control your own life? Do you really think you can move beyond your fears on your own knowledge and capacities?

THE FACE OF THE JUMPMASTER

We have good reasons why we are afraid to look at the Lord.

When Moses approached the burning bush, God identified himself. "Then he said, 'I am the God of your father, the God of Abraham, the God of Isaac and the God of Jacob.' At this, Moses hid his face, because he was afraid to look at God" (Ex. 3:6). Moses turned away from God.

Gideon was terrified when he finally recognized his ethereal visitor. "When Gideon realized that it was the angel of the Lord, he exclaimed, 'Ah, Sovereign Lord! I have seen the angel of the Lord face to face!'

"But the Lord said to him, 'Peace! Do not be afraid. You are not going to die'" (Judg. 6:22, 23).

Jesus took Peter, James, and John up a high mountain. "There he was transfigured before them. His face shone like the sun, and his clothes became as white as the light. Just then there appeared before them Moses and Elijah, talking with Jesus" (Matt. 17:2, 3).

Peter, ever impulsive, wanted to build three shelters on the mountain. But as he suggested this to Jesus, a bright cloud enveloped them, and a voice from the cloud said, "This is my Son, whom I love; with him I am well pleased. Listen to him!" (Matt. 17:5).

The disciples reaction was instantaneous. "When the disciples heard this, they fell facedown to the ground terrified. But Jesus came and touched them. 'Get up,' he said. 'Don't be afraid'" (Matt. 17:6, 7).

In all these situations, the appearance of God was for the purpose of reassurance. In each case, God delivered a message of hope, love, and vision for the future. Yet every time, the men to whom God appeared were certain death was near. But why? Why were they afraid to look at God?

Perhaps the answers lie in ourselves and not in God's appearance. To masquerade our souls before other men is easy. They possess a one-dimensional outlook and cannot see our inadequacies unless we allow them to. After a time of hiding and acting, we even fool ourselves. But when confronted with the knowledge, purity, and eyes of God, the masks split open, and we're left with the sickening realization that we don't know anything.

But do we see ourselves as God sees us? No. We're afraid to look at him because he might say "Go!" and we feel inadequate to do what he wants.

We see ourselves as shapeless lumps of clay. God sees us as we will be when we're finished. Intricate shapes and sculptures. He sees the glaze of experience and life spread with a careful brush.

God knows our strengths, the heights we can attain, and our weaknesses. If he gives us the go command, it is because he sees the abilities we can't see and believes we can hit the target area. He turns to the pilot with a knowing smile that says, "If we can get her off the wing now, she might hit the target area."

"GO!"

My respect for Joni Eareckson Tada grew immeasurably as I read her book, *Choices, Changes*. She tells about a van that a church gave her to use in her Joni and Friends ministry. All she had to do was learn to drive it. In Los Angeles.

My mind traveled back several years, and I was fifteen again. Three giggly friends sat in the back seat of the "Student Driver" car, and a monotone instructor quietly ordered: "Please pull the vehicle into traffic."

I did. On the left side of the road. The girls in the back screamed, and even the instructor's voice reached pitches he only dreamed about.

Now, I wasn't stupid. At fifteen, I knew what side of the road to drive on. But in my panic, I just couldn't get there. In the quiet little town of Auburn, Washington, I was so afraid to pull onto the street, I got confused.

Even with two good hands and two good legs, the thought of driving in Los Angeles chills me. The thought of learning to drive there brings sweat to my brow. And yet Joni learned to drive a van. In Los Angeles. With a mouthstick and a joy-stick.

How did she do it? She is a woman who knows who her jumpmaster is. She knows he is qualified and cares about her. She looks at him, and when he says, "Go!" Joni leaps or wheels where he tells her to.

Was Joni afraid? Did she learn to drive devoid of fear? Joni's appendages are paralyzed, not her heart or her mind. Like anyone who scoots behind the wheel of a car for the first time, Joni must have felt fear. Part of learning to drive is moving beyond fear; overcoming it until you are in control of the fear as well as the vehicle.

WHERE ARE YOUR EYES?

David always knew where to look. He said, "My eyes are ever on the Lord, for only he will release my feet from the snare" (Ps. 25:15).

Where do you look for direction? Other people? People who have the same clay feet you have? Do you look in the mirror? Can you trust your own instincts? Are you frustrated by the self-protective impulses that keep you from the full life God has promised you? God stands in the open door of an airplane. He patiently waits while you take in the view. If you feel inadequate to respond to him once you do look, remember that he chose the parachute, he plotted the course, and his ultimate goal is to help you land as close to the target as you are able.

How do you convince yourself to look at the jumpmaster when all you want to do is hide? Talk to yourself. I do it all the time, and I haven't been locked up. Yet. I said four things to myself when my head refused to turn in the jumpmaster's direction:

1. *What am I doing here?* I tend to ask myself this question a lot. In this case, the answer was simple. Trying to fulfill a dream. I struggled with the fact that my desire to skydive had no spiritual significance.

Many people asked me, prior to the jump, "Why do you want to parachute?" I would have seen some surprised faces if I had answered, "Because God told me to."

To take my step of total commitment, I had to understand, accept, and hang on to my original reason to try it in the first place.

2. *Who would be the most disappointed if I backed out?* Me. Sure, my husband wouldn't be too happy that I paid ninety-two dollars for a ten minute airplane ride (they didn't even serve lunch), but he would talk to me again sooner or later. Yes, my three kids waited all day in the hot sun to see Mommy scream her way to the ground. But they get over things pretty fast. The hot dogs and ice cream thrilled them as much as watching me jump.

Yes, I would be the most disappointed. I haven't lived up to my own standards in many areas of my life . I wasn't the person I wanted to be. Spiritually, mentally, or physically. The step off the airplane was symbolic for me. A step of determination. My will over my instincts. I needed to know I could do it.

3. *Would I survive?* As a wife and mother of three children, the question of survival was unbearably important. I had to weigh the risk in light of my responsibilities. Not to mention the deep rooted desire to face another day. *Would I survive* actually translated into a deeper question: *Does the reward exceed the risk?* If the answer to that question is no, then I must re-evaluate the action.

I responded positively. I had passed my fear of spiders

onto my daughter, Nichole. Now I wanted her to learn something else. Go for it! Even if you're scared to death, GO FOR IT! Moses didn't lead the Israelites across an Egyptian tightrope by looking for a safety net. Gideon didn't defeat the Midianites riding in a chariot behind thirty-two thousand soldiers.

I have my own obstacles to master, my own enemies to conquer, and finishing the jump was just one of them. Was it worth the risk? Yes. For me, the reward, the goal, far outweighed the possibility of death.

4. *"Oh, Lord. Can I do it?"* This last question was breathed out loud.

The answer came immediately. "Yes."

No prose. No sermons filled my mind. Just a simple yes.

Try asking yourself these questions. If it helps, write the answers down on paper. When you come to the fourth question, ask it out loud. "Oh, Lord. Can I do it?" You'll find that without realizing it, you've looked at the Jumpmaster. And his answer is yes. He knows you better than you know yourself, and he wants you to finish what you've started. You've climbed all the way out of the airplane at three thousand feet. Don't give up now. Finish the jump.

TIME TO CONSIDER

It's easy to trip over good intentions in the pursuit of lofty goals. We watch our feet and hit a wall, or watch the runner ahead of us and stumble over his debris when he crashes. We can only attain the possibilities God has for us when we maintain a steady vision. Like David, we must say, "My eyes are ever on the Lord, for only he will release my feet from the snare" (Ps. 25:15).

Beyond Fear

1. When you are afraid, where is the first place you look for help?

2. How important is it to you to overcome your fears?

3. What are the risks you face?

4. What are the possible rewards or results if you overcome your fear?

5. Where do you envision God standing as you make decisions?

6. If you look at the Lord in your moments of panic, what do you see? How do you feel?

7. Can you let go? Why or why not?

8. What are you trying to hang on to?

9. Take an honest self-evaluation. Who mans the controls in your life? If it's God, do you ever try to grab the controls out of his hands? What happens?

8

...

Letting Go

The sound of the jumpmaster's voice penetrated my chilled brain. "Go, Michelle!"

My last and greatest doubt hung suspended in time. Could I let go of the airplane? Would I let go? My fingers tightened and my toes dug in. One step. One leap is all it would take and I would be totally, irreversibly committed. But oh, that step was a biggee.

Desperate determination swept through me. One thought took over. *Just let go.*

My reluctant fingers gave up their rights and responsibilities and released their grip. The wind grabbed and yanked me away from the small airplane step. I was alone.

For one prolonged second, I was suspended by silence.

Surrounded, penetrated, and cushioned by utter freedom and peace. Then peace gave way as exhilaration burst and flooded my veins. I did it! I let go!

I can't begin to explain the sense of complete freedom I felt as I dropped away from the plane. A number of responsibilities ahead would bring me safely to the horse pasture. But for a few moments I was free. All the training in the world means nothing without a step of commitment when you're not sure of the outcome. That one step unlocks potential. Freedom.

How do we let go?

LETTING GO OF THE UNCONTROLLABLE

Most parents share a common fear: the loss of a child. Like other parents, I assumed this fear with the birth of our first son, Jason. Along with the fear came the belief that if our son died, I would be unable to cope with the loss. I wasn't strong enough. I watched over Jason with a wary eye. In the middle of the night, I tiptoed into his bedroom and poked him as he slept. Every breath spelled relief.

One sunny afternoon my husband sent me off to relax alone. I eagerly anticipated the first two private hours that I'd had in two and a half months.

Gordon waved from the door with a bundled Jason in his arms. "Take your time!"

I drove away with this beautiful father-son picture fresh in my mind. The radio played familiar songs and I sang. In between songs a newscaster reported a recent plane crash. My mind skipped over most of the information. Then he described the services for two of the victims. A father and son.

"The body of the infant was placed on his father's chest and the casket closed. The mother watched silently

72

as they lowered her husband and son into the ground." The reporter's voice crackled and broke.

Another reporter carried on with the story, but I didn't hear it. My stomach recoiled as if I'd been kicked. The maternal relationship I shared with this unknown woman welled up and engulfed me with pain.

"God, I couldn't handle it! If either my son or husband died, I couldn't handle it!"

A soft voice soothed the back of my neck and caressed my hurt. "Michelle," he inquired, "if I asked for Jason as I asked for Isaac and Samuel, would you give him to me?"

My fist struck the steering wheel, and my mental feet came out from under me. Words wrenched themselves out of my heart. "Yes, Lord. But please don't ask!"

My soul was wrapped in peaceful solitude. I let go of Jason. My love for my blue-eyed boy was intense and consuming, but I let go. I gave up my fears and let God catch them.

No promises. The peace I felt didn't mean fear wouldn't creep into the back door of my mind. But when I felt the presence of fear, God gently reminded me that I gave Jason to him.

Five days after I let go, Jason, a healthy, happy baby, died. His tiny white casket lay in the palm of God's hand. I handled it. God gave and showed me strengths I never knew I possessed. But to receive the strength I had to let go of the fear.

THE FINAL ACT

You've learned the first steps in moving beyond fear:
1. *Admission.*
2. *Ground School.*
3. *Get out of your airplane.*

The fourth step is the toughest, easy thing you'll ever do.

4. *LET GO*. This is the point in your life and your experience with fear when you say, "I've done all I can do. I let go."

Queen Esther's philosophy was: "If I perish, I perish." She let go.

Letting go can be a physical release of the last vestige of security even if it occurs on a mental level. Your body often fails to distinguish between real material threat and psychological threat. The thought of certain possibilities or situations can cause a person to break out in a cold sweat. Even though there is no immediate or real danger.

Karen and Anne were having a quiet cup of coffee in Anne's bright kitchen. They were relaxed and laughed at a few old memories. But something wasn't quite right with Karen. Anne knew something was troubling her friend.

"Well, Karen," Anne prodded. "Will you tell me what's up? Or do I have to guess?"

Karen gulped. "I'd rather not talk about it."

Anne studied Karen for a few moments without saying anything. Karen's hands began to shake. Her face was flushed, and her lips tightened into a grimace.

"Karen?"

"It's Jerry!" Karen blurted. "I'm afraid he's having an affair!"

For the next half hour, Karen poured out her suspicions and fears. She had no proof. She even admitted that many of her frustrations were born of personal insecurities. She was afraid of something that might not even be true. But her body didn't know the difference between truth and circumstantial evidence. Her entire physical being was wound up and ready to spring.

Karen and Anne spent several hours talking and praying.

Since Karen had little control over her situation until her husband proved or disproved his involvement, Karen had to come to a point in her fears where she could let go or go crazy. She chose to let go. With her friend's support and help, Karen released her fears. She said, "I can't do anything about it at this point. I'll just wait and see."

As Karen went out the kitchen door, she turned to Anne. "I feel as though I've lost weight. Or taken a nap."

The mental act of abdicating her fears allowed Karen's body to step down from its battle station position.

As long as you maintain your grip on fear or insecurity, you have to go wherever your high-strung emotions take you. If I had held on to the wing strut, I would've had to go wherever the plane dipped or dived. If it crashed, I'd crash with it.

Jason would have died whether I surrendered my terrified grasp or not. In the case of Sudden Infant Death Syndrome, I couldn't have helped him even if I were a surgeon standing by his bed when he died. But God asked me to let go so I wouldn't die with him. God wanted me whole, and he wanted me to grow.

What have you tied yourself to? In old seafaring days, sailors tied themselves to the ship's mast during fierce storms. The rope was intended to keep them from being swept overboard by massive waves. The rope and mast gave the sailors a measure of security. But sometimes the ship went down to the bottom of the ocean, and the men tied to it went down too. Ships, ropes, and masts provided safety only as long as the boat was on the water. If you have tied yourself to anyone or anything except God, you are in danger of sinking.

HANNAH

Hannah had one basic fear. She was afraid she would

die without children. For the women of her time, barrenness was the epitome of shame and disfavor. If a woman could not bear a child for her husband, she was derelict in her most basic duty. She was ridiculed and pitied. And Hannah was barren.

Elkanah, Hannah's husband, loved Hannah unconditionally. His heart ached for her, and he constantly comforted her. But as year passed into year, Hannah's fears took over. She wept and was provoked until she wouldn't eat.

One evening, after Hannah and Elkanah had finished their supper, the pain became too much for her. Hannah went to the temple and began to pray. She wept aloud and poured out her anguish to the Lord "in bitterness of soul." Her silent prayer was so fervent and emotional that Eli, the temple priest, accused her of being drunk.

"Not so, my lord," Hannah replied, "I am a woman who is deeply troubled. I have not been drinking wine or beer; I was pouring out my soul to the Lord. Do not take your servant for a wicked woman; I have been praying here out of my great anguish and grief."

Eli answered, "Go in peace, and may the God of Israel grant you what you have asked of him."

She said, "May your servant find favor in your eyes." Then she went her way and ate something, and her face was no longer downcast (1 Sam. 1:15-18).

Hannah poured out her problems, her wants, her frustrations, her fears to the Lord. She let them go. "Then she went her way and ate something, and her face was no longer downcast."

How did she do it? How do we stop worrying about

something when it's all we can think about? Hannah and Karen shared a common secret. They poured out their worries. All of the pain and doubt boiled to the surface, and they let it all spill over.

It hurts to spill your guts. Fear and anxiety can become such an integral part of our lives that it hurts when we finally rip them out and let them go. Sometimes the only way we know for sure we've allowed the surgery is because of the healing pain and itch.

What amazes me most about Hannah was her ability to let Samuel go. He was the fulfillment of her hopes and dreams. The child she was afraid she would never have, she let go. She told Eli, "I prayed for this child, and the Lord has granted me what I asked of him. So now I give him to the Lord. For his whole life he will be given over to the Lord" (1 Sam. 1:27, 28).

Hannah couldn't have returned Samuel to God if she had tied all of her hopes, all of her faith, all of her life around her son.

Hannah, at the weakest point of her life, poured her heart out to God, then let go. Then, in the best part of her life, when her hopes were fulfilled, she had the strength to be weak and let go.

STEP BY GRUELING STEP

Do you face object fears? Fear of cats, dogs, closed spaces, crowds? Is your battle with the fear of possibilities? Car crashes, airplane accidents, bears in the woods? Are the fears that plague you vague feelings and anxieties about things that might happen? Do you have panic attacks you can't explain?

You can take every step outlined in this book, or any other book, and it won't free you from fear. Not unless you learn to let go. It's a decision. Not an easy decision, but a conscious one, nonetheless. We can let go of our fears in many different ways. Not everyone lets go in the same way. One of the following methods may help you when you make your resolution:

1. *Esther's way.* Pray and fast, then say, "If I perish, I perish." Time and study helped me to understand what sounded like a flippant phrase. *Didn't Esther care whether she lived or died?* She cared. But what she was saying was "I'll worry about the axe when I see it fall" (Michelle paraphrase). Jesus said it simply: "Who of you by worrying can add a single hour to his life?" (Matt. 6:27).

How many of us subtract hours from our lives in the wasteland of worry? I do.

Esther had a job to do, and fear of death was keeping her from it. The only way she could accomplish what God had for her to do was to let go and hand the possibility of death over to God.

2. *By fire.* The pastor in a small church I attended challenged the congregation with an exercise in letting go. "Tonight," he announced, "I'll give you each a piece of paper. Write your strongest fears, your greatest worries on this sheet of paper."

The church was silent as minds wandered over troubles and trials. Heads were bent as a sound like a massive pencil scraping over paper whispered through the sanctuary.

After fifteen minutes, the pastor stepped up to the pulpit. "I want you to bring your paper down to the altar and pray about what you've written. God wants you to talk to him. He's available for you."

The altars were filled and people began the flow of pain and worries. We stayed at the altars until faces were mopped and smiles replaced anguished frowns.

The pastor wasn't finished. "There is a final step. Take it with me. I prayed about my fears, my anxieties, and now I want to be done with them. We can't take them home with us."

From the shelf in the pulpit, Pastor Drake pulled out three large coffee cans and matches. He struck one of the matchsticks and as it flared, he held it under the corner of his paper. Flames licked up toward his fingers and he dropped it into a can. "These concerns are no longer mine. I give them up. Can you burn up what you've prayed about tonight?"

The pastor was giving us a method for the physical release of intangible problems. It was symbolic and very therapeutic.

3. *Close your eyes and plug your nose.* I used to play a little psychological game with myself. My family lived in an apartment complex with a swimming pool. Swimming was great, once you were in the water and used to the temperature. The obstacle was to get into the water. First I tried going in little by little. Up on tippee-toes, my elbows in the air like a strange breed of water fowl, I semi-bounced deeper and deeper into the cold water. With every inch of goose-pimpled advance, a squeal broke through my chattering teeth. With this method, I usually got used to the water about the same time my mother told me it was time to get out.

Then I discovered my mind game. I stood on the diving board, closed my eyes, plugged my nose, and went for a walk. Oops! I stepped off! Well, too late to change my mind now. Within minutes I was acclimated to the water and having fun.

I am learning to walk off the springboard of worry and fear. I'll worry about the water when I hit it.

OPTIMISTS AND PESSIMISTS

Someone told me a joke in junior high that has stuck

with me all my life. I'll try to relay it to you in as near its original form as I can.

Two child psychologists compared methods of treatment and diagnosis. The first doctor said proudly, "In only two days I can tell you if a twelve-year-old male subject is happy or not."

The second doctor puffed out his considerable chest and put his thumbs behind his jacket lapels. "Ha! I can test a boy that age for fifteen minutes and tell you whether he is an optimist or a pessimist!"

"Impossible!" his friend responded.

"Bring me two boys, twelve years of age, and I will show you," the second doctor promised.

The next day, the first doctor brought in two males, both twelve, and stood them before his esteemed colleague. "Here are the subjects. Now show me your test!"

"Very well." The second psychiatrist took the two boys down a hall and sent them into two dark rooms with the promise that he would return in fifteen minutes.

The time passed quickly. Both doctors looked at their pocket watches and nodded. "It's time," said the doubting healer.

The two men approached one of the doors. The door opened easily and the light was on. It was a wonderful room, filled with so many splendid toys, the doctors had trouble finding the boy. They had to follow the mournful weeping and wailing that flowed from a corner of the room. In the corner, the boy sat with more than a hundred toys piled on his lap and body. His arms embraced and clutched many of them.

"What are you doing?" the first doctor asked, surprised. "Why on earth are you crying with so many beautiful toys around you?"

"Because I know someone is going to take them away

from me!" the young man blubbered.

The second doctor looked at the first with one eyebrow raised. "This is a pessimist."

The two doctors left the room and went down the hall. It took both of them to open the door to the second room. As the door gradually opened, a horrible smell assaulted their senses. The light was on in this room also, and it revealed a horrible sight. The room was filled three feet deep with horse manure. In the middle of the room the second twelve-year-old pursed his lips in a cheery whistle, and with a pitchfork, doggedly threw the manure to one side.

"How can you stand it!" the astounded skeptic asked through his plugged nose. "How can you be so happy in this filth?"

"Are you kiddin'?" the optimist replied. "Man alive, with all this stuff, there's got to be a pony in here somewhere!"

TIME TO CONSIDER

The boy in the room of toys never got a chance to enjoy his good fortune. He was too tied up worrying about how long the toys would be in his possession. If he could have let go of some of the toys, he would have had time and freedom to play. But he sat in misery.

Look around you. Are you happy in your room? Are you so worried about losing what you have that you can't enjoy what is around you? Then let it go. Enjoy it.

When I finally let go of the airplane, my fears dropped faster than I did. They disappeared below my feet. The parachute opened above my head, and I began to play. I played with the wind and sky. The three minutes it took to reach the ground were an incredible lifetime of joy.

Beyond Fear

1. Why did God ask Abraham to sacrifice Isaac?

2. Pretend you're Moses. God has just made a path through the Red Sea. A ferocious east wind is howling in your ears. God commands, "Go to the other side." What questions come to your mind?

3. What does the Lord want you to let go of?

4. Think about the two psychologists and their theories. What kind of room would you say you are in? What are your first reactions to the contents of those rooms?

5. Will you let go of your airplane? Why or why not?

9
...

I Blew It!
I Got Back into
the Airplane!

"I can't do it!" Bill shouted to Jon, the jump instructor who watched from the door of the aircraft.

"You can, Bill!" the instructor encouraged. "Just let go! It's easy! Let go!"

Bill's arms shook violently and his teeth chattered. He closed his eyes and willed his hands to let go. But he stayed where he was.

"Please!" he cried. "I'm going to be sick!"

But Bill's words were carried away by the wind. Jon could see his face, though. Bill wasn't going to let go. This is where a jumpmaster's job gets tricky.

Jon took a few moments to evaluate Bill's situation. "Bill," Jon yelled over the noise of the airplane. "Are you sure you can't jump?"

Bill's answer came in the form of a quick convulsion, and he fulfilled his promise to be sick.

"Okay, Bill! Take it easy. Are you done?"

Bill nodded weakly.

"Bill, look at me!" Jon wanted the frightened man to come back into the airplane on his own power. But Bill kept his eyes screwed shut and clutched his chest against the wing strut.

"I'll help you, but you have to move. Can you hear me?"

Bill nodded again.

"Good! Now move back toward the door. Keep a hold on the strut, but come back to the door!" No response.

Jon tried again, louder. "Look! This is what we're gonna do! You're going to come back to the door. I'll help you get back in the cabin, and we'll both go down in the plane."

Still no move.

"Do you want us to land with you out there?"

Bill's eyes flew open and he looked at Jon.

"Hey, Bill, that's great! Now c'mon! Let's get outta here! Just come toward me."

Bill slid his left foot over two inches. Then the right foot. Jon saw the lump in Bill's throat as he forced a swallow. One hand moved on the strut.

"Good! You can do it!"

Inch by terrible inch, Bill moved closer to the main body of the aircraft. Jon braced himself and grabbed one of Bill's arms when he came within reach. "Okay, buddy. When I tell you to, I want you to turn and back into the cabin. Get ready. I've got you! Now!"

With one good heave the bulky chute-pack cleared the door and Bill was in the cabin. Bill, Jon, and the pilot all released the air trapped in their lungs.

"Hey, guy!" Jon grinned. "Welcome back!"

Keen fear and utter disappointment flared in Bill's eyes.

He put his arms across his knees and rested his clammy forehead against his arms. "I couldn't do it."

The return flight was quick and quiet. As the small plane descended toward the runway, Bill lifted his head without opening his eyes. "I don't suppose we could land somewhere else?"

Jon's smile was sympathetic. "No. 'Fraid not."

BUMPS AND BRUISES

Defeat is devastating to the ego. Painful. Humiliating. And it happens to all of us. Praise the Lord! I have a tough time relating to people who rarely suffer defeat.

Here's a confession: I even have a personality clash with a certain disciple. I hope it's not a sin, but we just don't get along very well. I like him. He's a great writer, and I know God used him and spoke to him in a rare and beautiful way. But when I see him in heaven, I'm going to ask him, "Did you ever fail after you became a Christian?"

The people in the Bible failed. Not that we should use them for an excuse. But I can look at these people in the low points of my life and say, "You mean *he* blew it? Hey, if God didn't give up on him, maybe there's hope for me!"

The process of moving beyond fear is long and hard. In some areas you will have instant victories. But at least seventy-five percent of the time, you'll move four steps forward and two steps back. You'll fall. Sometimes you'll go back into hiding.

As a Christian teenager, I made some dumb mistakes. But I had a wise and caring older friend. One morning I came to her with a problem. She listened quietly while I told her how disappointed I was in myself.

"It was so dumb!" I cried. "I thought I was beyond this. How could I do something so dumb?"

Mrs. Skidgel took my hands in hers. She looked me full

in the face. "Michelle, you fell down. When you fall, you get scraped up a bit. But if you stand back up, you're usually one step farther than you were before."

Mrs. Skidgel changed my ideas about failure. She taught me by example to avoid a fall if possible, but when I found myself on the ground, I could learn.

A person who leans against a wall with arms folded across the chest never falls. The only people who fall down are the ones who are moving; going someplace. Are you willing to place yourself in dangerous or shaky situations, knowing you might fall?

GOD'S RESPONSE

Since God created us and knows our weaknesses, it shouldn't bother him when we crawl back into our airplanes. Right? Shouldn't he expect us to fail?

Yes, God does know our weaknesses. But we don't have to depend on our own strength. All possibilities are within our grasp when we reach for his hand, his knowledge, and his spirit.

Yet we do fail. We get scared and retreat. Our slumped shoulders and defeated sighs actually bring pain to the heart of God.

The disciples were consistent in their doubts and their failures. Jesus was with them for three years, teaching, loving, training them. When Jesus performed miracles, they had front row seats. When he raised Lazarus, Jesus was happy for the opportunity to increase their belief. "So then he told them plainly, 'Lazarus is dead, and for your sake I am glad I was not there, so that you may believe. But let us go to him' " (John 11:14).

The men who followed Jesus loved him and worked diligently for him, but they also let him down sometimes. In the storm on the lake, the disciples panicked: "The

86

disciples went and woke him, saying, 'Lord, save us! We're going to drown!' He replied, 'You of little faith, why are you so afraid?' Then he got up and rebuked the winds and the waves, and it was completely calm" (Matt. 8:25, 26).

Peter didn't have a plane to climb back into, but he probably looked around for a boat as he sank beneath the waves. Was Jesus disappointed? "You of little faith," he said, "why did you doubt?" (Matt. 14:31). The picture in my mind is of Peter climbing back into his boat, ashamed and embarrassed.

When Jesus taught with parables, he might have felt like we do in telling a good joke to someone who says, "I don't get it." The disciples often said, "Explain the parable to us."

Did Jesus get frustrated at their lack of understanding? Matthew 15:16 rings with frustration. " 'Are you still so dull?' Jesus asked them."

In the hour Jesus needed his friends the most, they let him down. He took three of them with him to the Garden of Gethsemane to pray. There, he confessed his pain. Then he said to them, "My soul is overwhelmed with sorrow to the point of death. Stay here and keep watch with me" (Matt. 26:38).

He craved the love and companionship of his friends. He told them so. He moved a short distance away, then returned a few moments later. He found his three friends sound asleep. He didn't hide his hurt. "Simon," he said to Peter, "are you asleep? Could you not keep watch for one hour?" (Mark 14:37).

Jesus understood the weaknesses of his human friends. "The spirit is willing, but the body is weak," he said. Yet, it still hurt that his friends couldn't stay awake while he was in agony.

ETERNAL OPTIMISM

When we crawl back into our airplanes and turn our backs on God's help, he is disappointed. He's sad. But he doesn't give up. Jesus never sat one of his disciples in a corner with a pointed "dunce" cap. No matter how much he felt like it.

As Peter walked on water, he reached out and Jesus grasped his hand.

God has never given up on anyone. He waits patiently in the doorway of the airplane. When he sees we can't jump, he helps us back in for a time. He wants you to make it. He yearns for you to take that leap of faith. But he still holds out his hand when you say, "I can't."

The only catch is you find yourself flying the same pattern in a couple of days. He'll make you try again. He'll keep setting up opportunities for you to complete your jump.

The Lord believes in you. Even when you don't believe in yourself.

During my freshman year in college, the local school district called me about a job. The man on the telephone told me the job involved special education, a field in which I was interested. The district needed a tutor. I agreed to an interview for the next afternoon to meet the student.

My nerves tingled as I walked the hollow school hall. I found the right room, took a deep breath, and exhaled. As I opened the door, I wished I had held my breath. My student had cerebral palsy. His disability was severe and my immediate reaction shamed me. *Oh, Lord! I can't do this!*

I stayed long enough to put on a show of interest, then escaped, my heart in my feet. I went straight back to the dorm, where it was safe, and cried. *I can't do it, God! I'm not ready!*

For several hours, I argued with God. Then I called the district office and turned down the tutoring job. I felt so small I could have walked under my Volkswagon.

For two days, God ministered to my defeated spirit. "I'll only give you jobs you have the strength for," he said. I kept waiting for a call from a pillow factory.

The call that came was from the school district. "I wondered if you'd changed your mind," the superintendent said.

My affirmative answer enrolled me in God's college. In the next six months I learned more about courage, determination, laughter, and life than I had learned before or since. I tutored academics. Merc, my student, tutored me in gutsy living.

When Merc was born, his parents were told to put him in an institution and let him die. "He'll be a vegetable. He'll never walk, talk, or think. He's less than human."

Merc's parents wouldn't give up. By the time I met Merc, he was twenty-one and in the eighth grade. He was an incredible math whiz. He walked. He used a letter board to communicate with people who couldn't understand his speech.

Merc taught me about falling. The first time I saw him fall, I had a heart attack. But he sat on the floor laughing so hard he couldn't talk. Finally he pointed to his letter board, "My legs want to go in different directions."

I am so glad God never gave up on me.

TIME TO CONSIDER

Okay, you gave up. You slipped back into the airplane. It's not a good feeling. But not the end of the world, either. Not unless you never fly again. Bill, the jumper at the beginning of the chapter, flew again. He climbed out of the airplane seven times, and seven times he climbed right back in. He got pretty good at it. But his jumpmaster stayed with him.

Jon figured anybody willing to go through it all seven times was bound to jump sooner or later. After every disappointment, Bill slumped in despair. And Jon slumped next to him.

But on the eighth try, something happened. Bill let go.

When Jon saw Bill drop away, a shout exploded from his mouth. He watched the red silk of the parachute flare out and form a perfect rectangle. Then Jon jumped and opened his own parachute. The two men bellowed and laughed all the way to the ground.

Bill's victory was Jon's victory. Your eventual victory is God's victory. He's willing to stick with you until it happens. He may experience a little disappointment once in a while, but his sadness is for you. He wants you to get past your fears. He knows you can, and he'll be there when you do.

1. When was the last time you disappointed God? Yourself?

2. How did your failure affect your relationship with the Lord?

3. What did you learn from the experience?

4. Why do we repeat the same mistakes?

5. How can we change the patterns?

6. Are you ready to jump again? When?

10

...

Fearless Freddie

You did it! You read the first nine chapters of this book. You used the suggestions and looked straight into the eyes of your greatest fear. Armed with knowledge and step by step procedures, you conquered your fear. Another fear pops its ugly head up and cackles at you. But hey! You throw on a purple cape and black mask. Ta da! You're "Fearless Freddie"!

"I can handle this, I've done it before," you say in your deep baritone voice. Then—crash!—head first into incredible danger—and you fall flat on your face. Your nose is broken and bloody, your cape is shredded and a front tooth is chipped. What happened?

You were arrogant. One victory does not win a war. Two victories won't win a war. There is a give and take in battle lines. Battles will be won and battles lost. The key to real and lasting victory is to win as many skirmishes as you can. And never give up.

Arrogance usually leads to loss. It did for me in one battle I waged against fear. I became pregnant three months after my son, Jason, died. My first response to the positive pregnancy test was jubilation. The second, third, and fourth responses were fears. *Will this baby die? Could I love another baby as much as I loved Jason? Was I a bad mother?*

My obstetrician sensed my fear during one of my checkups. He sat on a chair across from me and cleared his throat. "Michelle," he began gently, "are you sure you're ready for this? Maybe it's too soon for you to have another baby. Would you like me to do an ultra-sound?"

I stared back at him for a moment, thoughts flying through my head. *An ultra-sound? For what? If we found deformities, what would I do?* A decision formed in my heart as I searched my brain for intelligible words.

"No." My heart was pounding. "No. I don't need an ultra-sound. I am scared, Dr. Weiss. I'm scared stiff. But I know it's natural for me to be afraid, under the circumstances. I'm not going to let fear control me or how my baby is raised."

During the pregnancy, I repeated those words to myself a thousand times. Three weeks before Nichole was due, I contracted food poisoning. I spent half my energy convincing the hospital staff that I wasn't in labor, and the other half saying to myself, "It's okay. It's natural to be afraid. But fear is not going to control me. This baby is God's."

After Nichole's birth, I found it difficult to approach her crib. My fingers tingled, and my heart sat heavily in my stomach. The familiar words ran through my mind and past my lips. "It's okay. It's natural. But this is God's baby. I won't allow fear to control me." Every time I said these words, calm spread outward from inside my rib cage. I tackled fear one episode at a time. Day by day, God helped me deal with and conquer my fears.

I used the same process with my next son, Gordon. This time was easier. Fear attacked, but because I'd dealt with and conquered it before, I more confidently faced it this time. The old words carried me through my son's infancy.

By the time my daughter, Devon, was born, I felt like a veteran. I had needed to mentally prepare myself before Nichole's and Gordon's births. But when Devon came along I was cocky. After all, I'd made it through the tough time with Nichole and Gordon without fear getting the best of me. I was over it.

I made no mental preparation. I said no prayers for the Lord to remind me who my children belong to. I neglected to ask for strength or guidance. I donned my cape and mask, ready to fly on my own power.

My flight was cut short. A few days after Devon was born, I walked toward her crib. "Oh, God!" I yelled. "She's not breathing!" I grabbed a blanket off her, which prompted an extreme startle reflex. Instantly, arms and legs went straight out; her mouth opened wide in a soundless, terrified scream. *I* scared *her*!

I couldn't swallow for an hour. This was just the beginning. For the next two months, I lived in constant panic. Sometimes the fear was so thick that I couldn't bear to look in her bed. Then I'd send my husband to look.

One night, I lay in bed, wide awake. I waited for Devon's next breath while I held my own. Instead, through the fog, I heard God's whisper, "Michelle. If I asked for Devon as I asked for Isaac, Samuel, and Jason, would you give her to me?"

Oh, God!

I heard something cracking. My heart, mind, and self-reliance cracked and crumbled under the weight of God's question. They fell in pieces at his feet. The Lord scooped up the fragments and held them tenderly. "I'll take good care of her."

"Will you take her from me?"

No answer.

"Will she live?"

No answer.

"Yes, Lord. I'll give her to you."

I slept well that night. So did Devon. It was the first night she slept all the way through. At six a.m. she woke up and "asked" for breakfast. Every morning for the past two and a half years, Devon has asked for breakfast. And lunch. Dinner. Snacks. Treats. She loves to eat.

I almost missed out on God's strength because I tried to fly on my own. Without a change in me, my daughter's childhood would be miserable. I was well on the way to being an over-protective parent. SIDS would not have smothered Devon. I would have.

A HIDDEN KING

Saul is remembered for many things. His great stature. The battles he won. The insanity he suffered at the end of his reign. Few people realize just how shy, how afraid Saul was before he became a king.

The moment the prophet Samuel laid eyes on Saul, the Lord told him this was the man he would anoint king of Israel. In the middle of a casual conversation about some lost donkeys, Samuel dropped a bombshell: " 'And to whom is all the desire of Israel turned, if not to you and all your father's family?'

"Saul answered, 'But am I not a Benjamite, from the

smallest tribe of Israel, and is not my clan the least of all the clans of the tribe of Benjamin? Why do you say such a thing to me?' " (1 Sam. 9:20, 21).

Do those words sound familiar? Gideon and Saul shared the same family and the same fear. But the Lord told Samuel to anoint Saul as king, which Samuel did in a private ceremony. I think Saul more or less went along with the first ceremony to humor old Samuel.

When the time came for the public ceremony, Samuel informed the people of Israel that God had chosen a king for them. With great flourish he introduced the new king. But one little problem arose. Nobody could find Saul. "Finally Saul son of Kish was chosen. But when they looked for him, he was not to be found. So they inquired further of the Lord, 'Has the man come here yet?'

"And the Lord said, *'Yes, he has hidden himself among the baggage'* " (1 Sam. 10:21, 22 italics added).

Get a clear picture here: A man is running for president of the United States. A huge election party is thrown in his honor.

The campaign manager walks up to the podium. "People! I'm here to introduce your candidate for president of the United States. This man will deliver us from our economic difficulties. Our enemies will throw down their guns and run at the mention of his name. Under his leadership our country will grow and prosper! I give you the next president of the United States!" The campaign manager throws his arm out in a dramatic sweep across the stage and the crowd explodes with applause. But no one appears on stage.

"Uh, Tom." The campaign manager forgets about the microphone in front of him as he talks to the coordinator. "Where's the president? I told him to be here!"

"Oh, he's here, sir," Tom says, shifting his feet. "He's

hiding behind the baggage rack."

Would you vote for him?

A CHANGE OF HEART

Saul was the man God chose to rule the world's most obstinate nation of people. He was so afraid of his destiny and incredible responsibilities, he hid behind the baggage.

But Saul grew accustomed to his new role. With each victory over his fears, Saul grew in self-confidence. He got cocky. He took matters into his own hands.

The Israelites were faced with an enormous army of Philistines. Three thousand chariots, six thousand charioteers, soldiers as numerous as the sand on the seashore.

When the men of Israel saw that their situation was critical and that their army was hard pressed, they hid in caves and thickets, among the rocks, and in the pits and cisterns. Some Hebrews even crossed the Jordan to the land of Gad and Gilead.

Saul remained at Gilgal, and all the troops with him were quaking with fear. He waited seven days, the time set by Samuel; but Samuel did not come to Gilgal, and Saul's men began to scatter. So he said, "Bring me the burnt offering and the fellowship offerings." And Saul offered up the burnt offering (1 Sam. 13:6-9).

As long as Saul was shy and afraid he waited for the Lord's help and guidance. But Saul's position went to his head. He was impatient and took over Samuel's duties. He offered up the burnt offering to the Lord. He didn't understand what God really wanted.

Saul thought his victory in battle depended on the

Lord's pleasure in burnt offerings. But God longed for obedience. Saul made the same mistake again following the battle with the Amalekites. God told him to destroy the Amalekites and *everything* that belonged to them. But Saul took Agag, the Amalekite king, prisoner, and saved the calves and lambs for a sacrifice to the Lord.

The Lord spoke through Samuel without mincing words.

Samuel said, "Although you were once small in your own eyes, did you not become the head of the tribes of Israel? The Lord anointed you king over Israel. And he sent you on a mission, saying, 'Go and completely destroy those wicked people, the Amalekites; make war on them until you have wiped them out.' Why did you not obey the Lord? Why did you pounce on the plunder and do evil in the eyes of the Lord?" (1 Sam. 15:17-19).

At first, Saul replied defensively, "But I did. . . ." But then, in the same breath, he explained why he didn't obey God's command: "The soldiers took sheep and cattle from the plunder, the best of what was devoted to God in order to sacrifice them to the Lord your God at Gilgal" (1 Sam. 15:21).

In defending himself, Saul did three things:

1. *He pretended that he'd done what he was told.* In his heart Saul knew he'd goofed. But he tried to bluff his way out of his mess.

People love to bluff. Saul reminds me of the guy that parachuted into a backyard a mile away from the jump site. He was still wadding up his chute when his instructor caught up with him.

The instructor was happy to see the jumper in good

shape, but he had one question. "Why didn't you jump when you were told?"

"I did . . . the wind carried me away," the wayward man defended himself. The jump instructor knew the truth and rolled his eyes.

2. *He tried to side-step blame.* The Michelle paraphrase of verse 21 is, "If blame is to be placed, put it on the soldiers who took the sheep and cattle and stuff. . . ."

Saul knew he was in trouble so he shared responsibility with his soldiers. Men trained to obey his commands. But earlier, before he knew he had a problem, Saul took full responsibility for the victory. He set up a monument in his own honor and when Samuel found him he said: "The Lord bless you! *I* have carried out the Lord's instructions" (1 Sam. 15:13).

To accept full responsibility for our actions is hard. Especially actions of arrogance. I think Saul actually meant well, deep down, but he second-guessed God. He came right back to the original sin and asked himself, "Did God really mean it?" Then when he guessed wrong, he tried to blame someone else.

3. *He tried to justify his disobedience.* "The best of what was devoted to God, in order to sacrifice them to the Lord your God at Gilgal" (1 Sam. 15:21).

In essence, Saul's case was built on this: "But I did obey! Okay, my soldiers took a few things too good to pass up, but we were going to give them to the Lord."

The Lord saw through Saul. He knew the root of Saul's problem. Samuel said to Saul:

Does the Lord delight in burnt offerings and sacrifices as much as in obeying the voice of the Lord? To obey is better than sacrifice, and to heed is better than the fat of rams. For rebellion is like the sin of divination, and arrogance like the evil of idolatry. Because you have rejected the word of the Lord, he has rejected you as king (1 Sam. 15:22, 23).

THE REAL PROBLEM

Saul's big mistake was not the burnt offering. Nor his excuses or cover-ups. Saul's real problem was his arrogance. He felt strong enough, wise enough, to jump on his own without looking at the Jumpmaster. His parachute still opened; he still landed. But he was so far off course, he never found his way back again.

In my skydiving course, the instructor, Ted, told us about the fatal accident of a man who held the world record for the most free-fall jumps. He had made somewhere in the neighborhood of fourteen thousand jumps. One Saturday, before a large crowd, this man fell to his death.

"The man was killed by pride," Ted told the quiet class. "He was proud of the fact that in more than fourteen thousand jumps, he had only pulled his reserve chute three times. And all of those pulls were under five hundred feet. He was more afraid of ruining his record than losing his life."

Too much fear makes us cower and keeps us from doing God's will. No fear at all fools us into thinking we can handle life and all its twists by ourselves.

As I read through 1 Samuel, I had an odd sensation. I missed Saul. Not the king, but young Saul who simply wanted to find his donkeys. The man who hid behind the baggage because he was afraid to be king.

I understood the sadness in 1 Samuel 15:35, "Until the day Samuel died, he did not go to see Saul again, though Samuel mourned for him. And the Lord was grieved that he had made Saul king over Israel."

A similar verse is found in Genesis 6: "The Lord was

grieved that he had made man on the earth, and his heart was filled with pain" (Gen. 6:6).

God truly wants you to conquer your fears. He wants you to accomplish great and wonderful things. He wants you to fly and feel the freedom of riding the winds upon his will. But without his power under your wings, your flight will be extremely short and the landing rough.

THE CRAM SCAM

Sometimes arrogance causes us to jump without proper instruction and guidance; other times, it's ignorance. The result is the same.

Once in a while, we feel confident right up to the last minute, and then the fear returns. Suddenly we're faced with our inadequate preparation and a sense of doom takes over. Every college student understands this phenomenon.

Sally thought she was prepared for the final exams at the end of the month. "I never missed a lecture. I've got all my notes. I read the material."

Assured, she spent the month in the student center and with her friends. But the night before the exams, amnesia struck. Sally realized she didn't know the material as well as she thought.

"Where's the Vivarin?" she shouted down the hall to other frantic studiers. A popcorn popper sent out tendrils of fragrant temptation. Throughout the dormitory, a semester of knowledge was crammed into brains in a matter of hours.

Night passed as swiftly as the turning of pages. Bright sunshine filtered through the shaded window. Sally lifted her head where it had fallen on the desk and pulled at the scrap of paper stuck to the side of her face.

"What a mess!" she muttered as she surveyed the bits

of popcorn and notes scattered across the floor.

Then she remembered. "Finals! I gotta go to class!"

Sally flew into action. Within an hour she was dressed (one brown sock, one black) and in her seat for the first class. A slight buzz played in her head, but she hoped it was from all the information she'd injected into her brain.

The professor's assistant passed out the tests. Sally took her copy and began to read. She slunk down in her seat as her eyes scanned the questions, and she realized she could answer about half of them. She'd have to guess the rest.

"Help me, Lord," she prayed under her breath.

Bewildered by the questions, exhausted by her all night vigil, Sally did poorly on the tests. She learned the hard way that cramming doesn't work. It didn't work in college, and it doesn't work in life after college.

TIME TO CONSIDER

God wants you prepared for the challenges ahead. You can't "cram" the night before a crisis. The only way to prepare is to study. Study the scriptures, study people, and study the Lord. He wants you to overcome your fears so you can move beyond them. But he doesn't want you so self-confident you have no need of him.

1. What is spiritual arrogance?

2. Why did God choose Saul as king? Was it for his looks? His family? His wisdom?

3. What was Saul like before he became king?

4. What was he like after he became king?

5. What changed him?

6. What causes us to feel pride or arrogance?

7. Why do we trust ourselves more often than we trust the Lord?

8. Do you "cram" spiritually in the midst of crisis? How can we specifically plan ahead for fear and difficulties?

9. How did the Lord feel about Saul's self-reliance?

10. What color is your cape and mask?

11

...

The Trip Down

The lessons were drilled in well. In the ground class, we repeated the same process at least fifty times. "Jump, arch your back, then count! One thousand one, one thousand two, one thousand three, one thousand four, one thousand five, one thousand six! Check your parachute! If it's up, catch your brakes. If it's not up or it's tangled, perform emergency procedures."

I jumped. *What now? Oh yeah, arch your back. Okay, my back's arched. Now what? Count. Okay. One thousand one, one thousand two . . . help! I'm being jerked around like a hyperactive yo-yo! This isn't supposed to happen! Oh, it's my parachute. Heh heh. But I didn't count to six.*

Let's see, what's next? Look up and check for tangles.

103

Nope, no tangles. Just a nice green rectangle. Hey! I'm alive!

The most difficult steps of my skydive were behind me. But my job wasn't over. The parachutes most commonly used these days are actually called sails. They consist of two large rectangles joined together by cells that catch and allow the wind to flow through. Traditional style chutes were round and caught the air up underneath while slots at the back of the parachute allowed the air to flow out through the back.

The new parachutes give the jumper more control. By using two lines called brakes, the jumper makes turns and can slow his parachute down considerably.

More control invariably means more responsibility. The jumper must make enough turns in the right direction to land in the target area. My target was a horse pasture, but during the day, I watched fascinated as experienced jumpers aimed for a target eighteen inches in diameter. *If they can land on that little dot,* I thought, *I shouldn't have too much trouble finding a horse pasture.*

Now, here I was, hanging in the air, searching the miles of ground exposed beneath my feet for a giant neon-orange arrow. Since no arrow showed in the direction I faced, I prepared for my first turn. I gripped the brake with my left hand and pulled it all the way down until my fist was on my thigh. The parachute tilted and swung me around until I faced the east. *Ah! The arrow. I'm not lost. That's a good sign.*

The arrow was there to direct me according to wind patterns and to keep me in the general target area. A man stood at one corner of the fifteen foot long arrow, ready to run it around to indicate the direction I should turn.

He kept busy. First he ran right, then left. Then all the way around. Oops! Back the other way. Right then left.

Left and right. A curious bird tried to follow me and got airsick.

The ground came closer and closer. *Oh, man! I gotta land this thing!* I could hear people cheering for me. My husband and kids. The other jumpers from my class. Then the arrow man stepped in front of my descent.

He signaled for me to prepare to brake the parachute. I kept both arms straight up in the air, waiting for my last command.

"Flaaaaaare!" he shouted

With all the strength I had left in my arms (which wasn't much), I pulled down on both brakes. The outside edges of the parachute came down and formed a barrier against the wind. For a brief moment I was pulled up, then softly lowered into a mess of weeds on my posterior.

If you want status, you land on your feet. If you are happy just to be alive, you don't care which part hits the ground first.

"I did it!" I screeched in someone else's soprano voice. Then I collapsed. I couldn't believe it. Even though I looked like a meatball tied to a plate of green spaghetti, I couldn't believe I actually jumped out of an airplane.

NEVER ALONE

I wanted to hug my jumpmaster, but since my husband was still running the video camera, I decided against it. I wasn't just happy, I was grateful. I could never have parachuted alone. What began as a dream in the back of my fevered mind developed into a project for many people.

I wanted to skydive. Instead of telling me I was crazy, my husband said, "Do it!" In fact, when I would have let the idea slide, my husband challenged me to call and get information for the class. Then he urged me to sign up for the class.

Beyond Fear

When I arrived the day of the jump, I entered the classroom without knowing anyone in the class. But within a couple of hours, I felt comfortable with all of them. You can't have too many pretensions dressed in bell-bottom jumpsuits and motorcycle helmets. We all looked the same: goofy.

Something else bound us together. Fear. We all faced the same tremendous step, overcoming our fears. We were all shakey and pale, but more than one person said to me, "This is great! We can do this!"

Our instructor encouraged and challenged us. He was realistic about the possibility of failure and injury, but I knew he believed in us.

The jumpmaster played a huge part in my little victory. He told jokes. I would have smiled, but I was afraid my face might crack. I found comfort and encouragement in his humor, and I needed all the comfort I could find to help me relax.

The man on the ground ran five miles to keep me pointed in the right direction and out of other people's backyards and swimming pools. Can you imagine the embarrassment of landing in someone's swimming pool? It has happened.

I needed all of these people in my battle against fear. Especially the pilot. You can't skydive without a pilot to fly the airplane.

In every battle I've had with fear, someone has supported me. We all need help to face our fears. Most of us would rather face problems like characters in a war movie; a machine gun clutched under one arm, a strap of bullets thrown over the shoulder, and a foot-long knife strapped to a leg.

We would shoot up everything that stands in our way, then face the spotlight and sing, "I Did It My Way."

If you've tried to handle fear alone, you know it doesn't take long for reality to set in. God never intended for you to fight all by yourself. Some decisions you alone must make, but a friend or a qualified counselor nearby to support your decisions may make the difference in success and failure.

If you think it's you against the world, maybe you need to look around. The Lord promised never to leave us alone.

WHERE IS MY FRIEND?

Kids on a playground are so fun to watch. Without even thinking about it, they illustrate biblical principals. I stood one day outside a chain link fence watching some children play one of my old favorites, red rover.

Giggling and laughing, shoving and pushing, they chose up two teams. The teams spread out in two long lines and faced each other about thirty feet apart. Then the old sing-song started.

"Red rover, red rover, send Jacob right over!"

The brave Jacob stepped out in front of his line, pawed the ground once or twice with his foot and charged like a miniature bull. The receiving team set themselves for the impact of Jacob's hurtling body. The whole line joined together, hand to elbow, and formed a human bungi-cord.

Jacob's shooting body struck the line between two slight boys. A collective grunt arose, and the line of children shifted a step or two. But Jacob could not break through. He hung for a moment over the boys' arms, then stood and turned to face his own team with an embarrassed grin. He took his place with his new team.

These children had probably never read Ecclesiastes or understood how God's principles affect their lives. Yet they were living examples.

Two are better than one,
because they have a good return for their work:
If one falls down,
his friend can help him up.
But pity the man who falls
and has no one to help him up!
Also, if two lie down together, they will keep warm.
But how can one keep warm alone?
Though one may be overpowered,
Two can defend themselves.
A cord of three strands is not quickly broken
(Eccles. 4:9-12).

As one team lost more and more players, it lost its ability to resist the onslaught of running children. But the link with many kids on either side was strong and resilient.

I needed people on both sides of me as I jumped. You need people on both sides of you to overcome your fears.

So where are your friends? They're usually close by, hands out waiting for you to link up. But they can't do a thing for you unless you're willing to grab their hand and hold on for dear life.

Sometimes this means asking for help. A friend of mine commented one day; "I *hate* asking anyone for help!" Her nose wrinkled up as though the idea smelled bad. "I can't do it!"

Some people have little difficulty asking for help. But for most of us, the confession that we can't make it on our own comes only after barbaric torture.

Debbie waited too long to grab for help. She woke up one morning and found herself in a hospital. Her arms were strapped down and both wrists heavily bandaged. When her vision cleared enough to look around the room, she saw an old friend sitting beside the bed.

"Debbie?" Carol jumped up when she saw Debbie open her eyes. "You finally woke up. I've been waiting, praying you would wake up."

Debbie stared at Carol's face. It was Carol, but she looked funny. Her make-up was smeared all over the place, and her eyes were red and swollen. Debbie felt Carol touch one of her hands.

"Oh, Debbie, what are you doing here? Why didn't you tell me? I know now what you've gone through, with John leaving you, your job, your kids. But why didn't you tell me?"

"How do you admit your husband loves someone else, and your daughter ran away? When your car breaks down and you lose your job, how do you call someone on a bright and sunny day and say, 'Hi! I want to kill myself. Do you mind?'"

Carol put her hands on her hips, looked straight at Debbie, and said, "You pick up the telephone, dial my number, and say, 'Carol, I've got a problem. Can we talk?'"

Contrary to common wishes, other people cannot read our minds. If you need help, ask for it. Ignore the voices in your head that say, "I'll be a burden. People don't want to hear my problems. They only like me when I'm happy and fun."

Those thoughts are wrong. Not stupid, just inaccurate. A real, two-sided friendship only exists when both people are needed. You may be the kind of person who always listens to other people's problems but never shares any of your own. You are cheating your friends. They should feel you need them as much as they need you. If that isn't the case, you have an unbalanced friendship.

TRAINING CAMP

Right now, as you read this book, you may be having a stare-down with fear. You know how important the element of encouragement is to you in your efforts to win the contest. When you finally do land in the mess of weeds on your posterior, you may have accomplished a personal goal, but you haven't reached the end. A circle is involved.

Just as you needed help wiping the sweat off your brow, someone not far away is waiting for a clean handkerchief. You have received encouragement, now it is time for you to encourage someone else.

Everyone who cheered me on in my skydiving endeavor (with the exception of my husband and children) understood the panic I faced in the doorway of the airplane. They understood because at one time they stood there too. They had earned the right to make jokes, slap my back, and say, "I know you can do it!"

When you conquer your particular fear, you earn the right and the responsibility to help others overcome their fear.

Paradoxically, many people are afraid to be encouragers. A certain amount of risk is involved. The person you try to help may reject your hand.

What if they don't want your help? What if you say or do the wrong thing? All of a sudden you face a whole new set of fears.

These kinds of fears are especially common when you are considering approaching someone who has recently experienced extreme loss. I have lost a child through death, yet the thought of talking to a grieving mother scares me. I do it, but I have to chop my way through a jungle of fears first.

In her book, *The Gift of Encouragement*, Gloria Chisholm tells one way to work through anxiety as we attempt to encourage someone.

> In deciding to gain victory over any fear, we need to hold in front of us the proverbial carrot-in-front-of-the-donkey. In this case, it's not what we will gain, but what others will lose if we remain in our fearful state.
>
> You are needed. Because of the unique places you've walked and the personal trials you've suffered and your fresh perspective on life's experiences, you can offer what no one else can. So don't allow fear or self-consciousness to stop you from motivating others, from pushing them onward and upward, from moving them closer to God.[1]

As you work your way through the mazes and tunnels of your own fear, savor the feelings. Even the awful ones. When you've made it to the other side of the maze, go back to the starting line, and you'll find someone else in your place. You can give them an idea of the obstacles ahead. You can say with complete authority, "Hey, it's tough. *But you can make it!*"

I got my start in professional writing by going to a writers' conference. The thought of approaching an editor terrified me. Fifteen minutes after I arrived at the conference, one of the editors approached me and started a conversation. She really seemed to care about me, a green (forest green) writer, at her first conference. I was more than encouraged. I was elated.

Later in the week I had another opportunity to talk with this editor and she made a revealing comment, "I remember how I felt at my first writing seminar. I thought the editors were like gods. I want writers, all writers to feel comfortable with me."

That editor not only encouraged me, she became a close friend and steady mentor. Knowing she had once been as in awe of editors as I was eased my apprehensions. Now she was an editor and her genuine interest lifted me about ten feet above ground.

THE PILOT

One person encouraged me more than any other the day I parachuted. He didn't say a word. He never touched me. I can't even tell you what he looked like. Actually, I was trying so hard to keep my knees from sounding like castanets, I never took a good look at him.

My pilot. The most comforting thing to me as I rode the wide blue yonder was that someone was controlling the plane. He sat quietly in his chair. His full concentration was on the instruments in front of him and the ground far, far below. We never spoke. But he seemed to know what he was doing, so I didn't ask any questions.

You and I have a great Encourager. He sits behind the controls and flies around in circles until you find the courage to get out of the plane. And he never runs out of gas.

God wants you to understand: he didn't bring you all the way up to three thousand feet to see you make a fool out of yourself. He brought you here for triumph. For conquest.

He believes in you when everyone else thinks you're crazy. He believes in you when you think he's crazy. Admit it. Sometimes you think God's crazy.

The first time it became evident God wanted me to speak in public, I said, "God, you're crazy! I can't do that! I get the warbles talking to more than three people at a time!"

112

He didn't strike me with lightning. I believe God loves to prove us wrong. He uses our "can'ts" to show us his "cans."

My one regret after the parachute jump was that I couldn't even remember what my pilot looked like. I didn't think about thanking him as we parted company, and I wouldn't recognize him now.

Take a good look at your Pilot. Study his face and expressions. When you land, you'll want to find him and tell him how much his guidance and care meant to you. You'll have other flights ahead of you, and if you know your Pilot and have confidence in him, some of the turbulence dissipates.

TIME TO CONSIDER

Hezekiah, whose very name means, "Yahweh is (my) strength," had a distinct vision of the Pilot's face. He loved the Lord with a passion that had long been absent in Israel. He ordered the destruction of idols and Asherah poles. Under Hezekiah's reign, the walls of Jerusalem were repaired, and the doors of the temple reopened. Hezekiah turned the eyes of Judah back to the God of David.

When most of the repair work was done in Jerusalem, Hezekiah began to build up the army of God.

He appointed military officers over the people and assembled them before him in the square at the city gate and encouraged them with these words: "Be strong and courageous. Do not be afraid or discouraged because of the king of Assyria and the vast army with him, for there is a greater power with us than with him. With him is only the arm of flesh, but with us is the Lord our God to help us and to fight our battles." And the people gained confidence from what Hezekiah the king of Judah said (2 Chron. 32:6-8).

Hezekiah's faith was rooted in his ability to see beyond fact. Beyond Sennacherib, the king of Assyria. Beyond his own fears. His ability to see God in difficult circumstances made it possible for him to encourage a nation of rebellious and fickle people.

Hezekiah had moved beyond his fears. But he didn't sit down in the road and say, "Whew! Boy, am I glad that's over." He turned around, went back the way he came, and encouraged others to move on. To look at the Pilot.

That is the challenge. Sometimes we fight such fierce battles against personal fears that we become self-absorbed. We pass people by who need our help. Either we don't notice them, or we're too busy with our own struggles. It's too bad we grow up. We quit playing games like red rover and get wrapped up in solitaire. We don't have, nor do we offer, the resiliency of linked arms and fixed feet.

Look at your hands. Are they empty?

1. Look back at fears you've managed to overcome in the past. Who helped you?

2. Besides the Lord, who has had the greatest affect on your life for good?

3. What did that person do for you?

4. How can you use your experiences with fear to encourage someone else?

114

5. Let's talk about short-term goals. The Pilot has been flying you around for a while now, and he wants you to get ready to jump. Look down. What would you say is his general target area for you? Where is he asking you to land?

6. What will you do once you land?

7. Most people are visually oriented. We carry mental images of people we've never met and are often surprised by their actual appearance. What is your mental image of God?

8. Is the image of God you have now the same as it was a year ago? If not, how has it changed

12

...

Covered by the Arms of the Cross

It would be wonderful if I could say I've overcome every fear I've ever had. Wonderful but not true. I've worked out the fear of spiders. They still disgust me, but I don't run anymore.

I am happy to report I haven't stalked through my house with any knives for a long time. Baseball bats don't count, do they?

The Lord has helped me categorize my fears and deal with them accordingly. The first category is the boot camp for overcoming fears. It's called, "Camp Ittlgetcha." This "boot camp for conquerors" is filled with mostly object fears and fears of possibilities.

I have worked through most of these. Somewhere along the line I developed the attitude: "If I'm afraid of it then I'll do it!"

An example is my fear of snakes. When I was in a mall and saw a sign that read, "Have your picture taken with a boa constrictor," I couldn't resist. I got in line. A short line.

By now, you know my standard responses to fear. Palpitating heart, swollen throat. Sweat. The shakes. They were all there.

I watched, mortified, as the person in front of me took his turn with the snake. I laughed nervously when the snake's trainer had a little trouble unwinding the snake after the picture was taken.

The camera operator stepped up to me. "Your turn. Just sit on the stool over there, and Rob will help you with the snake."

"Okay," I squeaked.

I perched myself on the small stool and tried not to flinch as the trainer positioned the thick body of the boa across the back of my shoulders. "How big is he?" I asked in a raspy voice.

"Oh, he's pretty small for a boa constrictor. He's only about six feet long."

This "small" reptile put enough weight on my shoulders that I had to lean forward to keep my balance on the stool. "He won't squeeze me, will he?" I tried to pretend I was kidding.

"Oh, no. He's too short." He continued to drape the surprisingly soft snake around my shoulders. "Hold him here please." The trainer positioned one hand under a loop. "And here, right behind his head."

"His head? Do I have to?"

"Yep."

He took my hand and showed me how to hold the snake, right behind the head. The trainer moved away.

Can snakes' eyes bulge? They must be able to, because when the trainer glanced back at us, he kind of jumped.

"Hey! Not so tight! Loosen your grip!"

The flash bulb popped, and the snake was unwrapped from around me. He was probably as relieved as I was. But I felt great. I had done something I never thought I could do. I grabbed the snake's tail. And his body. And his head.

Boot camp helped me overcome many similar fears. It was always hard, sometimes fun.

I'm still working on the second category of fears. These are emotional fears that run deep and affect me in ways I'm only beginning to realize. These are the snakes I run from.

But one by one, God is making me reach down with my trembling hand and grab a tail. I'll tell you the truth. I hate it. I would rather hold a dozen real snakes and jump out of ten airplanes than deal with some of the writhing pythons from my past.

Yet in the middle of my struggle, the Lord is leading me to a new place in my life. I've known Jesus for more than seventeen years, but I have never visited his home. His refuge for me. In this last year he has handed me a ticket. My ticket to freedom and safety. The writing on the ticket says:

Therefore, since we have been justified through faith, *we have peace with God through our Lord Jesus Christ, through whom we have gained access by faith into this grace in which we now stand. And we rejoice in the hope of the glory of God.* Not only so but we also rejoice in our sufferings, because we know that suffering produces perseverance; perseverance, character; and character, hope. *And hope does not disappoint us, because God has poured out his love into our hearts by the Holy Spirit, whom he has given us* (Rom. 5:1-5 italics added).

FAITH TO BE STILL

Much of this book has been devoted to inspiring movement. "Get out of your airplane." "Make the step of commitment." "Get up, move out, get going."

Conversely, sometimes we need to sit still to overcome our fears, times when fear has invaded every fiber of our being and our soul cries out to bolt and run.

In the eye of your terror, a voice will tell you, "Be still, and know that I am God; I will be exalted among the nations, I will be exalted in the earth. The Lord Almighty is with us; the God of Jacob is our fortress" (Ps. 46:10, 11).

It's almost like assisting the knife-thrower. The skilled marksman of cutlery displays his talent with a bull's-eye target. Or he splits fruit fastened to a tree. But what is the true testament to his abilities? The person willing to stand, outlined as a target, with a smile on her face.

The assistant watches the knife as it flies towards her head. One flinch, one small movement could spell graphic disaster. The only remedy is to be still. To trust the thrower.

The audience gasps as the knife strikes the board a scant inch from the assistant's face. Then applause fills and rolls through the air. "Bravo! Bravo!"

The Master receives glory because the assistant was still.

Can you hold still when you're racked with fear? Can you trust the Lord long enough for the knife to miss you?

THE VOICE IN THE STORM

How do you know when to move and when to stay

put? You listen. You stand with Elijah in the cave on Mount Horeb, and wait. Elijah fled to the cave because he was afraid of Jezebel's anger. But as Elijah waited, the Lord paid a visit.

> Then a great and powerful wind tore the mountains apart and shattered the rocks before the Lord, but the Lord was not in the wind. After the wind there was an earthquake, but the Lord was not in the earthquake. After the earthquake came a fire, but the Lord was not in the fire. And after the fire came a gentle whisper. When Elijah heard it, he pulled his cloak over his face and went out and stood at the mouth of the cave.
>
> Then a voice said to him, "What are you doing here, Elijah?" (1 Kings 19:11-13).

Our human nature waits for thunder and lightning to signify God's guidance. Thunder grabs our attention and lightning makes a definite impact. But the way we usually hear from the Lord is through soft voices and whisperings. Sometimes we hear him in the voice of a child. Or an appreciated breeze on a hot day.

When you sit still long enough to hear him, he'll ask you the same question he asked Elijah: "What are you doing here?"

No recrimination or reproach is in the question. He wants to know what you think you're running from.

The worst nightmare I ever had involved my son, Gordon. He was only two at the time, and I had a vivid, horrifying dream in which he was harmed, and I couldn't protect him. I can still feel the groan that rushed through my body in the dream. It escaped through my lips and woke my husband. He started shaking me in an effort to bring me out of my nightmare.

"Michelle! Wake up! Come on, Michelle, you're dreaming!"

I could hear his voice, and slowly slid from my dream back to my bedroom. But my slashed heart stayed behind.

"What happened? What were you dreaming about?" my husband asked as he held me close.

"I don't want to talk about it. It was too awful." I couldn't stop shaking.

"Tell me about it."

For the next fifteen minutes I described my dream. With each word spoken out loud, the dream lost some of its power over me. By the time I finished my story, I had put the dream into perspective. My heart slowed to its normal pace, and I was relaxed enough to go back to sleep.

The Lord knew why Elijah was in the cave. He had sent for him and strengthened him for the journey. God knew exactly what Elijah was afraid of. But Elijah needed to put his fears into words in the presence of Someone who loved him. Someone who wouldn't say, "That's silly! Didn't I just perform a fantastic miracle for you in front of all Israel? What's the matter with you?"

God showed his love and concern for Elijah by bringing him into a place of refuge. He came to Elijah in a whisper and gave Elijah the strength and encouragement to go back down the mountain.

How do we know when the Lord is speaking to us? He's the gentle whisper that invigorates your tired soul.

WHERE ARE YOU?

Do night terrors rob you of sleep? Are you a chicken? Do you stand in the middle of your living room and cry out, "God help me, or let me die"?

Are you in a place where you can hear his voice? Listen. This is what the Lord wants you to hear: "The Lord your God is with you, he is mighty to save. He will take great delight in you, he will quiet you with his love, he will rejoice over you with singing" (Zeph. 3:17).

When I was a little girl, the most frightening place on earth was a cemetery. Especially at night. My family lived close to an old Indian cemetery in Montana, and my sister and I passed it on the way to and from school.

One night, my sister and I had to pass by the graves after dusk. Our feet dragged but our pulses raced. The sky grew darker and darker until all we could see of each other were the whites of our enlarged eyes.

We held hands so tight my fingers lost circulation. But I didn't complain. Suddenly, Cindy stumbled and fell. I couldn't see where she landed. "Cindy! Cindy! Where are you?" I begged.

A hand touched my arm and I screamed.

"Michelle! It's me, you goof!" Cindy took my hand again and we headed home.

I was frightened in the cemetery, but as long as Cindy held my hand, I could make it through. I couldn't stand the thought of being alone there.

Sixteen years later, I sat in the middle of a cemetery at three in the morning. I was afraid, but the grave I sat beside held no terror for me; it held my son's body. My hand brushed the top of dew-soaked grass, the coldness a part of me.

My fears were generated by a feeling of failure. I was afraid that my fight with my husband earlier that evening had severed our relationship. I was afraid that the Lord took Jason from me because I was a bad mother. I was afraid I would never have more children. I was afraid that the useful part of me had died and was buried in the grave beside me.

"God, where are you?"

"Where are you, Michelle?"

"I don't know, Lord."

"Where do you want to be?"

"Here with Jason. I should be here, not him."

"Jason isn't here, Michelle. He's with me, and so are you. Go home."

I took a deep breath, stood up, and went home. My husband and I talked and worked things out. I had three more children. (Not all of them that night.) The Lord has found so many ways to make me feel useful I sometimes throw up my hands and yell, "Hold it! Hold it!"

Once I knew where God was and where I belonged, I developed a sense of direction. Don't flounder around in your fears, soaking up the dew. Look for the Lord. He's nearby. Get a sense of direction and follow it. Your fears can't hold you back, only you can.

Where are you?

TIME TO CONSIDER

Two thieves were crucified with Jesus. One of the men insulted and taunted Jesus. The other man recognized the face of refuge. "Don't you fear God," he said, "since you are under the same sentence? We are punished justly, for we are getting what our deeds deserve. But this man has done nothing wrong."

Then he said, "Jesus, remember me when you come into your kingdom" (Luke 23:40-42).

Both men were afraid to die. But the second man had a perspective on fear. His fears were allayed by the man beside him, whose arms, like his own, were stretched wide on a wooden bar. Those arms wrapped around his soul and covered his heart. He found the only real refuge. The only real place of safety. And he found it while he hung on a cross.

It really doesn't matter where you are today. If you've locked yourself in your bedroom, in a closet, or in your own mind. It doesn't matter. God is with you no matter where you sit. You have already moved beyond fears that once bound you. It's a matter of perspective.

1. Where are you right now?

2. Where is the Lord?

3. Where was the Lord when Elijah needed him? Why did the Lord wait for more than forty days and nights to reveal himself and his plan to Elijah?

4. How does the Lord reveal himself to you?

5. If your perspective on fear has changed as you read this book, how?

6. Where do you want to be?

7. Are you ready to make your quantum leap? If so, don't forget the parachute. Trust the Pilot. Look at the Jumpmaster. And "GO!"

Source Notes

INTRODUCTION

1. Philip Yancey, *Open Windows* (Westchester, IL: Crossway Books, 1982), p. 75.

CHAPTER 3

1. John Haggai, *How to Win Over Fear* (Eugene, OR: Harvest House Publishers, 1987), p. 58.

CHAPTER 4

1. Miriam Adeney, *A Time For Risking* (Portland, OR: Multnomah Press, 1987), p. 108.

CHAPTER 5

1. Joyce Landorf, *Monday Through Saturday* (Waco, TX: Word Books, Inc., 1984), p. 35.

CHAPTER 6

1. Fulton J. Sheen, *Life of Christ* (Garden City, NY: Doubleday & Co., 1977), p. 321.

CHAPTER 11

1. Gloria Chisholm, *The Gift of Encouragement* (Lynnwood, WA: Aglow Publications, 1990), pp. 126, 127.

Support Group Leader's Guide

Issue-oriented, problem-wrestling, life-confronting—Heart Issue books are appropriate for adult Sunday school classes, individual study, and especially for support groups. Here are guidelines to encourage and facilitate support groups.

SUPPORT GROUP GUIDELINES

The small group setting offers individuals the opportunity to commit themselves to personal growth through mutual caring and support. This is especially true of Christian support groups, where from five to twelve individuals meet on a regular basis with a mature leader to share their personal experiences and struggles over a specific "heart issue." In such a group, individuals develop trust and accountability with each other and the Lord. Because a support group's purpose differs from a Bible study or prayer group, it needs its own format and guidelines.

Let's look at the ingredients of a support group:
- Purpose
- Leadership
- Meeting Format
- Group Guidelines

PURPOSE

The purpose of a Heart Issue support group is to provide:

1. An *opportunity* for participants to share openly and honestly their struggles and pain over a specific issue in a non-judgmental, Christ-centered framework.

2. A *"safe place"* where participants can gain perspective on a mutual problem and begin taking responsibility for their responses to their own situations.

3. An *atmosphere* that is compassionate, understanding, and committed to challenging participants from a biblical perspective.

Support groups are not counseling groups. Participants come to be supported, not fixed or changed. Yet, as genuine love and caring are exchanged, people begin to experience God's love and acceptance. As a result, change and healing take place.

The initiators of a support group need to be clear about its specific purpose. The following questions are examples of what to consider before starting a small group.

1. What type of group will this be? A personal growth group, a self-help group, or a group structured to focus on a certain theme? Is it long-term, short-term, or ongoing?

2. Who is the group for? A particular population? College students? Single women? Divorced people?

3. What are the goals for the group? What will members gain from it?

4. Who will lead or co-lead the group? What are his/her qualifications?

5. How many members should be in the group? Will new members be able to join the group once it is started?

6. What kind of structure or format will the group have?

7. What topics will be explored in the support book and to what degree will this be determined by the group members and to what degree by the leaders?

LEADERSHIP

Small group studies often rotate leadership among participants, but because support groups usually meet for a specific time period with a specific mutual issue, it works well to have one leader or a team of co-leaders responsible for the meetings.

Good leadership is essential for a healthy, balanced group. Qualifications include character and personality traits as well as life experience and, in some cases, professional experience.

Personal Leadership Characteristics
COURAGE

One of the most important traits of effective group leaders is courage. Courage is shown in willingness (1) to be open to self-disclosure, admitting their own mistakes and taking the same risks they expect others to take; (2) to confront another, and, in confronting, to understand that love is the goal; (3) to act on their beliefs and hunches; (4) to be emotionally touched by another and to draw on their experiences in order to identify with the other; (5) to continually examine their inner self; (6) to be direct and honest with members; and (7) to express to the group their fears and expectations about the group process. (Leaders shouldn't use their role to protect themselves from honest and direct interaction with the rest of the group.)

WILLINGNESS TO MODEL

Through their behavior, and the attitudes conveyed by it, leaders can create a climate of openness, seriousness of purpose, acceptance of others, and the desirability of taking risks. Group leaders should have had some moderate victory in their own struggles, with adequate healing having taken place. They recognize their own woundedness and see themselves as persons in process as well. Group leaders lead largely by example—by doing what they expect members to do.

PRESENCE

Group leaders need to be emotionally present with the group members. This means being touched by others' pain, struggles, and joys. Leaders can become more emotionally involved with others by paying close attention to their own reactions and by permitting these reactions to become intense. Fully experiencing emotions gives leaders the ability to be compassionate and empathetic with their members. At the same time, group leaders understand their role as facilitators. They know they're not answer people; they don't take responsibility for change in others.

GOODWILL AND CARING

A sincere interest in the welfare of the others is essential in group leaders. Caring involves respecting, trusting, and valuing people. Not every member is easy to care for, but leaders should at least want to care. It is vital that leaders become aware of the kinds of people they care for easily and the kinds they find it difficult to care for. They can gain this awareness by openly exploring their reactions to members. Genuine caring must be demonstrated; merely saying so is not enough.

Some ways to express a caring attitude are: (1) inviting a person to participate but allowing that person to decide how far to go; (2) giving warmth, concern, and support when, and only when it is genuinely felt; (3) gently confronting the person when there are obvious discrepancies between a person's words and her behavior; and (4) encouraging people to be what they could be without their masks and shields. This kind of caring requires a commitment to love and a sensitivity to the Holy Spirit.

OPENNESS

To be effective, group leaders must be open with themselves, open to others in groups, open to new experiences, and open to life-styles and values that differ from their own. Openness is an attitude. It doesn't mean that leaders reveal every aspect of their personal lives; it means that they reveal enough of themselves to give the participants a sense of person.

Leader openness tends to foster a spirit of openness within the group; it permits members to become more open about their feelings and beliefs; and it lends a certain fluidity to the group process. Self-revelation should not be manipulated as a technique. However, self-evaluation is best done spontaneously, when appropriate.

NONDEFENSIVENESS

Dealing frankly with criticism is related closely to openness. If group leaders are easily threatened, insecure in their work of leading, overly sensitive to negative feedback, and depend highly on group approval, they will probably encounter major problems in trying to carry out their leadership role. Members sometimes accuse leaders of not caring enough, of being selective in their caring, of structuring the sessions too much, of not providing enough direction, of being too harsh. Some criticism may be fair, some unfair. The crucial thing for leaders is to nondefensively explore with their groups the feelings that are legitimately produced by the leaders and those that represent what is upsetting the member.

STRONG SENSE OF SELF

A strong sense of self (or personal power) is an important quality of leaders. This doesn't mean that leaders would manipulate or dominate; it means that leaders are confident of who they are and what they are about. Groups "catch" this and feel the leaders know what they are doing. Leaders who have a strong sense of self recognize their weaknesses and don't expend energy concealing them from others. Their vulnerability becomes their strength as leaders. Such leaders can accept credit where it's due, and at the same time encourage members to accept credit for their own growth.

STAMINA

Group leading can be taxing and draining as well as exciting and energizing. Leaders need physical and emotional stamina and the ability to withstand pressure in order to remain vitalized until the group sessions end. If leaders give in to fatigue when the group bogs down, becomes resistive, or when members drop out, the effectiveness of the whole group could suffer. Leaders must be aware of their own energy level, have outside sources of spiritual and emotional nourishment, and have realistic expectations for the group's progress.

SENSE OF HUMOR

The leaders who enjoy humor and can incorporate it appropriately into the group will bring a valuable asset to the meetings. Sometimes humor surfaces as an escape from healthy confrontations and sensitive leaders need to identify and help the group avoid this diversion. But because we often take ourselves and our problems so seriously, we need the release of humor to bring balance and

perspective. This is particularly true after sustained periods of dealing seriously with intensive problems.
CREATIVITY

The capacity to be spontaneously creative, to approach each group session with fresh ideas is a most important characteristic for group leaders. Leaders who are good at discovering new ways of approaching a group and who are willing to suspend the use of established techniques are unlikely to grow stale. Working with interesting co-leaders is another way for leaders to acquire fresh ideas.

GROUP LEADERSHIP SKILLS

Although personality characteristics of the group leader are extremely significant, by themselves they do not ensure a healthy group. Leadership skills are also essential. The following need to be expressed in a sensitive and timely way:
ACTIVE LISTENING

Leaders need to absorb content, note gestures, observe subtle changes in voice or expression, and sense underlying messages. For example, a woman may be talking about her warm and loving feelings toward her husband, yet her body may be rigid and her fists clenched.
EMPATHY

This requires sensing the subjective world of the participant. Group leaders, in addition to being caring and open, must learn to grasp another's experience and at the same time maintain their separateness.
RESPECT AND POSITIVE REGARD

In giving support, leaders need to draw on the positive assets of the members. Where differences occur, there needs to be open and honest appreciation and toleration.
WARMTH

Smiling has been shown to be especially important in

the communication of warmth. Other nonverbal means are: voice tone, posture, body language, and facial expression.

GENUINENESS

Leaders need to be real, to be themselves in relating with others, to be authentic and spontaneous.

FORMAT

The format of meetings will differ vastly from group to group, but the following are generally accepted as working well with support groups.

MEETING PLACE

This should be a comfortable, warm atmosphere. Participants need to feel welcome and that they've come to a "safe place" where they won't be overheard or easily distracted. Some groups will want to provide baby-sitting.

OPENING

Welcome participants. The leader should introduce herself and the members should also introduce themselves. It is wise to go over the "ground rules" at every meeting and especially at first or when there are newcomers. Some of these would include:

1. Respect others' sharing by keeping what is said in the group confidential.

2. Never belittle the beliefs or expressions of another.

3. Respect the time schedule. Try to arrive on time and be prompt in leaving.

4. Feel free to contact the leader at another time if there are questions or need for additional help.

Many meetings open with a brief time of prayer and worship and conclude with prayer. It often helps to ask for informal prayer requests and brief sharing so that the group begins in a spirit of openness.

MEETING

Leaders can initiate the meeting by focusing on a particular issue (or chapter if the group is studying a book). It is wise to define the focus of the specific meeting so that the group can stay on track for the entire session. (See Group Guidelines below.)

CLOSING

Strive for promptness without being abrupt. Give opportunity for those who need additional help to make an appointment with the leader. Be alert to any needing special affirmation or encouragement as they leave.

GROUP GUIDELINES

Because this is a support group, not an advice group, the leader will need to establish the atmosphere and show by her style how to relate lovingly and helpfully within the group. Participants need to know the guidelines for being a member of the group. It is a wise practice to repeat these guidelines at each meeting and especially when newcomers attend. The following guidelines have proven to be helpful to share with support groups:

1. You have come to give and receive support. No "fixing." We are to listen, support, and be supported by one another—not give advice.

2. Let other members talk. Please let them finish without interruption.

3. Try to step over any fear of sharing in the group. Yet do not monopolize the group's time.

4. Be interested in what someone else is sharing. Listen with your heart. Never converse privately with someone else while another member is addressing the group.

5. Be committed to express your feelings from the heart. Encourage others to do the same. It's all right to feel angry, to laugh, or to cry.

6. Help others own their feelings and take responsibility for change in their lives. Don't jump in with an easy answer or a story on how you conquered their problem. Relate to where they are.

7. Avoid accusing or blaming. Speak in the "I" mode about how something or someone made *you* feel. Example: "I felt angry when. . . ."

8. Avoid ill-timed humor to lighten emotionally charged times. Let participants work through their sharing even if it is hard.

9. Keep names and sharing of other group members confidential.

10. Because we are all in various stages of growth, please give newcomers permission to be new and old-timers permission to be further along in their growth. This is a "safe place" for all to grow and share their lives.

Inquiries regarding speaking availability and other correspondence may be directed to Michelle Cresse at the following address:

P.O. Box 640
Roy, WA 98580